THE KORAN

AND

THE KAFIR

— ISLAM AND THE INFIDEL —

D1706364

THE **KORAN**
AND
THE **KAFIR**
— **ISLAM AND THE INFIDEL** —

ALL THAT AN INFIDEL NEEDS TO KNOW ABOUT THE KORAN BUT IS EMBARRASSED TO ASK

— A. GHOSH —

The author wishes to express his thanks. for permission to quote from the works listed below:

Sita Ram Goel, Story of Islamic Imperialism in India/Defence of Hindu Society/Hindu Society under Siege. Voice of India, New Delhi 1982

P.N. Oak, the Taj Mahal is Tejo Mahalaya - A Shiva Temple. Publisher: P.N. Oak, New Delhi

Colin Maine, The Dead Hand of Islam. The Rationalist Association of N.S.W. Australia

Every reasonable effort has been made to obtain appropriate permission to reproduce the copyrighted materials included in this edition. If notified of errors or omissions, the author and publisher will make the necessary corrections in future editions.

Publisher: A. Ghosh
               5720 W. Little York Suite #216
               Houston, Texas 77091

               ISBN 0-9611614-0-X

Printed in the United States of America

Contents

PREFACE

This book is intended for non-Moslems in general and Hindus, Buddhists, Jains, Parsees and Sikhs in particular. It is common knowledge that as a rule non-Moslems are quite ignorant of the contents of the Koran and the Hadis, the holy books of Islam. These books are the fountain springs of Islamic thought. The injunctions contained in these holy books direct the code of conduct of the Moslems, their social system and their notions of right and wrong, in short the main ingredients that go into the making of the Moslem psyche.

It is a compilation of information taken from already existing works by renowned scholars. The bibliography at the end indicates the sources. It is hoped that the book will generate enough interest among its readers so that they would get to the source material themselves and do some thinking of their own.

In the not so hoary past, the Moslems wielded their swords to weed out Christianity, Judaism and polytheism, to dethrone the gods of their neighbors and to install in their place their own godling, Allah. The recourse to imperialism under the garb of iconoclasm, slavery and slaughter, loot and raid, arson and murder that followed to establish an empire in the process, was another matter. These were incidental terrestrial rewards for disinterested celestial pursuits.

a) ISLAMIC REVIVAL

Thanks to the new found oil-riches, the old mission is being revived. A kind of Islamic Cominform is taking shape in Jeddah, Saudi Arabia. The 'nouveau riche' Arab is assuming responsibility for Moslems everywhere, looking after their spiritual needs as well as their more temporal interests. Their wealth is active whether it is in Pakistan, the Philippines, Bangladesh, Indonesia or Malaysia.

Arabs are still weak in arms and dependent on the West but the full fury of their interference is to be seen in the countries of Asia and Africa which are economically poor and ideologically weak. Here Islam works from the bottom as well as from the top.

Local politicians and members of the news media are bought. The conversion into Islam of the President of Gabon and the Emperor of the Central African Empire is a case in point. The Arabs have adopted the Moslem minorities of 'darul-Harb' (infidel countries that have not yet been subdued by Islam). The non-Moslem minorities of these countries are being tempted to accept Islam and thus gradually change these countries into 'darul-Islam' (countries where Islam reigns supreme in all walks of life).

b)   PROBLEM OF MOSLEM MINORITY

Even as it is, Moslem minorities are difficult to assimilate in the national mainstream of a country. The Arab financial and ideological support has made the task still more difficult. In India for instance, the Moslems were not the first foreigners to come and settle down in the country. In earlier times, the Greeks, the Scythians, the Kushans and the Huns had also come to India as invaders. By the time the Moslem invaders arrived, all these erstwhile foreigners had been fully assimilated in the native population and their cultures synthesised with the indigenous culture of India. There never was a Greek or Scythian or Kushan or Hun minority problem in India.

On the other hand, the Zoroastrians or Parsees came to seek refuge in India when the Moslem invaders attacked Persia and started wide-spread loot, arson and murder. The whole of Persia was forcibly Islamised and only those who could escape such as the ancestors of present-day Parsees of India, survived. The Parsees have remained a distinct minority group with their own characteristic culture. The Jewish minority of India had kept its racial and cultural identity intact for nearly two thousand years. There never was any problem between these groups and the native population of India, the Hindus. It is not necessary therefore for different racial groups to get assimilated or for different cultures to get synthesised before they can live in peaceful coexistence. It is only when a culture is intolerant, exclusive and aggressive that peaceful coexistence becomes impossible.

x

It is not in India alone that the indigenous population has found it well-nigh impossible to coexist peacefully with the Moslems. Greece had the same problem till it expelled its Moslem population. Yugoslavia and Cyprus in the West and the Philippines in the East have an unsolved Moslem problem till today. Spain has no Moslem problem because it did not allow any Moslems to remain within its borders after it defeated the invaders in a struggle spread over seven centuries. Russia and China have solved their Moslem problem for the time being in quite another way - by massive terror and ruthless suppression. One wonders how long the experiment would succeed.

On the other hand, no country where Islam has attained unrivalled power, has allowed any non-Islamic minority to survive. The Jews and the Christians were given the status of 'zimmis' by the prophet himself. But what has happened to them in the lands of their birth? The Jews have been finally cleaned up from all Islamic countries. The Christian minorities that managed to survive in Egypt and Lebanon are having a very hard time at the hands of the latest wave of Islamic fundamentalists supported by the oil-wealth. There are no Zoroastrians in Iran any more. The Baha'is are being butchered openly there today. The Hindus of Bangladesh are being herded and hounded out. The Sikhs, Hindus and Christians of Pakistan have already been reduced to microscopic minorities, well on their way to complete extinction. It is to be seen how long the Hindus and Buddhists of Bali in Indonesia and of Malaysia can survive the renewed offensive unleashed by petro-dollars.

c)   FALSE PRETENSE

Islam pretends that it stands for universal brotherhood and democratic equality as contrasted with sectarian divisions and class hierarchies rampant in other societies. But in reality, Islam had never put forward this pretension before the rise of democracy and socialism in modern times. The old theologians of Islam were meticulous in placing multifarious people in their proper places. The 'momins' (believers) constituted the master class ('millat') entrusted with the holy mission of imposing the prophet's faith and the laws of Islam on all mankind. The kafirs were the scum of the earth who were to be consigned to eternal hellfire whenever they could not be decimated by the 'momins'. The 'zimmis' were people who accepted the supremacy of the Islamic state and agreed to live as second class citizens under severe disabilities. The slaves were mere merchandise who could be bought and sold in the bazaar or 'souk' and killed without compunction with or without reason. And the women ('zan') were personal property comparable to gold and silver ('zar') and land ('zamin') and to be kept veiled and hidden in the harem if they happened to be legal wives, and circulated as gifts amongst the aristocracy if they happened to be concubines. Within the 'millat' itself, the 'Qurayza' had primacy over the plain Arabs at the start of Arab imperialism. The civil list devised by Caliph Umar for monetary grants given to Arab families out of the booty obtained in the raids on infidels reflects this class hierarchy in Arab society. As the Arab empire expanded east and west, the non-Arabs everywhere were treated as inferior people, in law as well as in practice, even when the latter became 'momins' (believers) by renouncing their ancestral faith. Later on, the Turks took over the Arab legacy of being a master race. Pakistan tried the same game in erstwhile East Pakistan, now Bangladesh, but was not successful. Islam has never known any brotherhood or equality even within its 'millat'.

A typical Moslem is patient, good-natured, but also volatile and excitable, naive and yet shrewd, married, with several children and sometimes several wives, supported by a deep trust in Allah as an unquestioning ally, possessed of a strong sexuality, not so educated and of an unthinking mind, proud of Islam's past glories achieved by the sword, devoted to relatives and yet prone to conflict, torn between traditions of the past and the new demands of today's world, proud of being a Moslem without a precise idea of what it really means, surrendering to any mullah without criticism, yearning for a life of leisure as depicted in Islamic folklore and hateful of the kafirs for his own inadequacies, and contemptuous of others' religions and ways of life.

d)   THE KAFIR'S LOT

The great sage Swami Vivekananda, founder of the Rama

Krishna Mission had said:

> 'Under the Mussulman rule, the king himself was the supreme priest; he was the chief guide in religious matters; and when he became the emperor, he cherished the hope of being the paramount leader in all matters over the whole Mussulman world. To the Mussulman, the Jews or the Christians are not objects of extreme detestation; they are, at the worst, men of little faith. But not so the Hindu. According to him, the Hindu is idolatrous, the hateful Kafir; hence in this life he deserves to be butchered; and in the next, eternal hell is in store for him. The utmost the Mussulman kings could do as a favor to the priestly class (meaning Hindu Brahmins) - was to allow them somehow to pass their life silently and wait for the last moment. This was again sometimes considered too much kindness! If the religious ardor of any king was a little more uncommon, there would immediately follow arrangements for a great Yajna[1] by way of Kafir-slaughter!'

e) THE KORAN AND THE MEIN KAMPF

Hitler had written his autobiography Mein Kampf many years before he became Germany's Chancellor. His philosophy and plans were clearly spelled out in his book in all seriousness. He did not hide the fact that his mortal enemy was France, that he desired to annihilate the entire Jewish people, that he wanted to expand the Reich or the German state by taking over Eastern Europe, that he considered the communists the scum of the earth. His objectives were not hidden from the public; anyone interested in finding out the true nature and the implications of Hitler's objectives was free to do so from his open book. But most did not even bother to read his book and thus remained ignorant of many facts concerning them. The few who did, were not heeded to. As a result, disaster after disaster followed; millions died before the world woke up. At terrible cost to humanity, Hitler was eventually overthrown.

The Koran's exhortations to the believers to annihilate the kafirs, to confiscate their land and property, to enslave their women and children are for anyone who cares to read the book. The 'jihad' or the holy war is supposed to be waged incessantly until all the kafirs are decimated and the whole earth taken over by the followers of Islam. The methods have been amply illustrated throughout history. The Crusades, the annihilation of the Armenians, the Jews and the Bengali Hindus in East Pakistan are well-known. There is no reason to believe that the objectives of Islam have undergone any modification in recent years. Islam denies any means to its followers to purify itself. It is considered to be in a state of purification achieved by the prophet and all the measures of purification are already enunciated in the Koran and the Hadis, Islam's holy books. Thus Islam forbids any reformation of the prophet's religion. Reformers[2] are forbidden in Islam. The injunctions of the Koran are final and will remain valid for ever and the believers must surrender themselves to its dictates as explained by the mullah in power, Khomeini or anyone else. Power is the key word.

f)   PRECEPTS AND PRACTICES

IT IS UP TO THE KAFIR TO MAKE HIMSELF AWARE OF THE MESSAGE OF THE KORAN. THE KORAN HAS A LOT TO SAY ABOUT HIM. This book highlights episodes from history both old and new, as examples of Islam in action. The excerpts from the Koran indicate the precepts of Islam. One is thus provided with the opportunity to reconcile the practice of Islam with the precepts. The precepts of Islam flow from the Koran, the recitation of the words of Allah and the practice is exemplified by Islam in action throughout history.

The present book is in no way exhaustive. No doubt many readers will be able to cite more incidents than treated in this book, to prove the same point. The purpose is not to express contempt for the prophet's religion but to draw the attention of the non-Moslems, the kafirs and the 'zimmis' of the world, to a phenomenon very much in existence today but to which not much light has been shed. The contents of the book should therefore be judged primarily by the non-Moslems on the basis of their own perception of the phenomenon. It must be realised that Islam is imperialistic and politically motivated with religious overtones.

As ignorance in any form is to be avoided for greater comprehension, there should not be any reluctance on the part of the non-Moslems to learn more about the prophet's life, deeds and precepts. The prophet's personal life is an important aspect of Islam. Of all ignorance, the self-inflicted type is the worst. The holy books of Islam and those on Islamic history are easily available in many languages and there is absolutely no reason for misunderstanding to persist in the minds of kafirs.

Clearly, Islam is essentially hostile to other religions. The situation created by the new wave of Islamic fundamentalism not only in Islamic countries but in non-Islamic lands as well, is a phenomenon that demands close vigilance. This can only be achieved by learning the true nature of Islam. And learning the true nature of Islam can be very well done by the study of the Koran and accounts from world history. If the non-Islamic peoples must protect themselves from the onslaught of Islam, then they must pay more attention to what Islam really has in mind as far as the non-Moslems are concerned.

The question is NOT how evil the Moslems are. They may have bad smell and beat their grandmothers and wives regularly. The question is: Can we keep them from beating OUR grandmothers and wives?

The author has been inspired in great measure by the works of renowned scholars such as Ram Swarup, Sita Ram Goel and P.N. Oak of India. Many historical incidents have been taken from the famous works of Late Sir Jadu Nath Sarkar as mentioned in the Bibliography. Thanks are due to the publishers of Colin Maine's article 'the Dead Hand of Islam' of New South Wales, Australia. The author is indebted to John G. Runion, Sr. and Victor G. Templeton for their help in the preparation of some of the text.

Footnotes

1. Yajna: Sanskrit word meaning 'great religious sacrifice'.

2. Very few Moslem intellectuals have dared to undertake any kind of reform of the prophet's creed to suit the changed circumstances. If they do, Islamic societies are sure to take revenge as happened in the trial of Sadiq Jalal al-Azm in recent years.

FOREWARD

The original Koran is written in Arabic of which most kafirs or non-Moslems have very little or no knowledge at all. There are many English translations by eminent scholars and these are readily available in the market. Three Korans have been consulted during the preparation of this book. The Koran by Mohammed Marmaduke Pickthall has generally been followed not because this is the best translation but because this is the edition that is most widely read by the Moslems of the English speaking world.

It is said that the prophet Mohammed was illiterate himself; but he was a great orator. His speeches have been collected by different scribes over the years and the Koran that is presented to the Arabic speaking world is the true source material. However, the Koran that has been followed in this book is a genuine and true translation of the Arabic Koran that is revered by the Moslem world.

In this book, only those 'surahs' and 'ayats' (chapters and verses) have been cited that refer to the kafirs or the infidels. There are many verses in the Koran that have nothing to do with the kafirs or infidels. Also, the verses presented are in no way exhaustive; there are many more kafir or infidel-related verses in the Koran conveying the same meaning or similar message for the Koran is somewhat repetitive in nature. The purpose of this book is to draw the attention of the kafirs or non-believers to the main thrust of the Koranic injunctions as far as non-Moslems are concerned.

The historical episodes have been taken from different parts of world history. However, a great majority of the episodes have been gleaned from Indian history which has been thoroughly documented by Hindu, Moslem and British historians of repute. In India, the world had the opportunity of witnessing an unfolding drama of Islam in action, a phenomenon which fills the heart of a Moslem with pride and glory but sickens the heart of a non-Moslem with utter frustration, hate

xvii

and contempt. The historical occurrences, had they been taken from chapters of European history under the Moslems would have the same effect in the minds of the readers. The idea is to analyse the message of Islam and its practice and how Islam influences human behavior.

Short descriptions of different aspects of Islam's social practices, generally unknown among the infidels, have also been treated in this book. The subject is vast and cannot be fully dealt with in a short compilation as this one. The bibliography provided will be helpful for those who are willing to undertake exploratory work for their own information. It must however be borne in mind that a translation from original Arabic into another language generally spoken by infidels sometimes loses many of the salient features of the original message. Pursuit of the truth has never been easy.

DEDICATED

TO THE THREE MILLION UNARMED AND INNOCENT
KAFIR MEN, WOMEN AND CHILDREN WHO WERE
BRUTALLY MURDERED BY THE MOSLEM ARMY OF PAKIS-
TAN, A DASTARDLY DEED THAT WAS EQUALLED BY A
BETRAYAL EPITOMIZED IN THE FREEING OF THE 90,000
RUFFIANS WHO COMMITTED UNLIMITED AND HEINOUS
CRIMES AGAINST HUMANITY, AND

TO ALL THOSE WHO HAVE COMMITTED THEMSELVES
NEVER TO FORGET.

CHAPTER 1

OF KAFIRS AND ZIMMIS

All non-Moslems are infidels. However, there are gradations. The people of the Book (meaning the Bible, both the old and the new testaments) are the Jews, the Christians and the Moslems. According to Islam, Mohammed was the last prophet and there would be no other future prophet or prophets. The Jews and Christians are considered as people of little faith by the followers of Islam. On the other hand, the Buddhists, the Hindus, the Jains, the Sikhs, the Zoroastrians, the Taoists, in fact, all other religions are considered as the religions of the kafirs. They are the worst of all and do not have the right to exist in this world unless of course they accept Islam unconditionally.

All the infidels living in an Islamic state are supposed to pay a special tax called the 'jiziya' which signifies their acceptance of the superiority of Islam. Such people are called 'zimmis'.

At one time the kafirs did not have the right of a 'zimmi', the second class citizen. He was to be slaughtered or forcibly converted into Islam. However, the Hanafi school of thought was in support of giving the rights of 'zimmis' to the Hindus, Buddhists and Jains as well as the Sikhs and other people who did not belong to the Book. All other Islamic schools of thought were against giving any right to the kafirs.

Ziyauddin Barani wrote: "If Mahmud had gone to India once more, he would have brought under his sword all the Brahmans[1] of Hind[2] who, in that vast land, are the cause of the continuance of the laws of infidelity and of the strength of the idolators; he would have cut off the heads of two or three hundred thousand Hindu chiefs. He would not have returned his Hindu-slaughtering sword to its scabbard until the whole of Hind had accepted Islam. For Mahmud was a Shafiite, and according to Imam Shafi the decree for Hindus is Islam or death - that is to say, they should be either put to death or accept Islam. It is not lawful to accept 'jiziya' from Hindus who have neither a prophet nor a revealed book."

However, the great number of Hindus in India made it impossible for the believers to kill them all and eventually even the Hindus had the 'good fortune' to be accepted as 'zimmis'. But to a Moslem such people have been and still are kafirs.

A Moslem jurist called Shaikh-ul-Islam had propounded the doctrine of 'din-panahi' during the reign of a Moslem king called Iltutmish. On the subject of the kafirs being treated as 'zimmis' he was of the opinion: "The kings should protect the religion of Islam with sincere faith... And the kings will not be able to perform the duty of protecting the faith unless, for the sake of Allah and the prophet's creed, they overthrow and uproot 'kufr' and 'kafiri' (infidelity), 'shirk' (setting partners to Allah) and the worship of deities. But if the total uprooting of idolatry is not possible owing to the firm roots of 'kufr' and the large number of kafirs, the kings should at least strive to insult, disgrace, dishonor and defame the Hindus, who are the worst enemies of Allah and the prophet. The symptom of the kings being the protectors of Islam is this: When they see a Hindu, their eyes grow red and they wish to bury him alive; they also desire to completely uproot the Brahmans, who are the leaders of 'kufr' and owing to whom 'kufr' is spread and the commandments of 'kufr' are enforced...Owing to the fear and terror of the kings of Islam, not a single enemy of Allah and the prophet can drink water that is sweet or stretch his legs on his bed and go to sleep in peace."

However, the fact is that the Moslem kings were no fools and knew better. The mullahs lived in a fool's paradise amidst leasure and luxury in towns protected by Islamic armies. They could very well issue injunctions from their ivory towers. The Moslem kings, on the other hand, had to live mostly on battlefields and could feel in their guts the power equations of a situation in which they had to wage a constant war against repeated Hindu reassertions of independence. They had discovered very soon that the Hindus hated Islam as a system of black barbarity and would fight rather than submit to this sinister creed. Moreover, they needed the Hindus for doing work which the mullahs and the swordsmen of Islam were neither equipped nor inclined to do - agriculture, commerce, industry, scavenging and so on. No wonder the Moslem kings fell for the Hanafi school of thought as soon as it was expounded to them, not because they liked this school of thought but simply because they had no other choice. They imposed 'jiziya' and other disabilities on the Hindus, and reduced them, wherever they could, to the status of hewers of wood and drawers of water.

The mullahs howled at this 'sacrilege'. They mourned: "Should the king consider the payment of a few coins by way of 'jiziya' as sufficient justification for allowing all possible freedom to the infidels to observe and demonstrate all orders and details of infidelity, to read the misleading literature of their faith and to propagate their teachings, how could the true religion get the upper hand over other regligions and how could the emblems of Islam be held high? How will the true faith prevail if rulers allow the infidels to keep their temples, adorn their deities and to make merry during their festivals with beating of drums, singing and dancing?"

Prophet Mohammed permitted the Jews and the Christians living in Islamic countries in those days, the right to survive as 'zimmis', if they refused to accept Islam. On that basis, one can separate the two kinds of infidels as follows:

'Zimmi':   'Nasranis' or Christians (this includes Catholics and Protestants of all denominations); and Jews.

Kafirs: Hindus, Buddhists, Jains, Sikhs, Zoroastrians, Shintos, Taoists and Animists.

It is true that the 'Ahmediyyas' or 'Qadianis' of Pakistan and the 'Shias' of Iran are sometimes called 'non-Moslems' by the 'Sunni' Moslems but that is a subject beyond the purview of this book.

Footnotes

1.   Brahmans: Hindu priestly class; Brahmins.

2.   Hind: India.

THE KORAN ON THE KAFIRS

The following are only a few of the important sayings from the Koran, dealing with kafirs or infidels. There are many more similar sayings throughout Islam's holy book. The message is the same. The numbers of chapters and verses are indicated in Roman and Hindu (or Arabic) numerals on the left. The injunctions are clearly spelled out so that there is no misunderstanding in the minds of simple believers.

VIII/12 : When thy Lord inspired the angels, (saying:) I am with you. So make those who believe stand firm. I will throw fear into the hearts of those who disbelieve. Then smite the necks and smite of them each finger[1].

VIII/36 : Lo! those who disbelieve spend their wealth in order that they may debar (men) from the way of Allah. They will spend it, then it will become an anguish for them, then they will be conquered. And those who disbelieve will be gathered unto hell.

IX/5 : Then, when the sacred months have passed, slay the idolaters wherever ye find them, and take them (captive), and besiege them, and prepare for them each ambush. But if they repent and establish worship and pay the poor-due, then leave their way free. Lo! Allah is Forgiving, Merciful.

IX/28 : O ye who believe! The idolaters only are unclean. So let them not come near the Inviolable Place of Worship after this their year. If ye fear poverty (from the loss of their merchandise) Allah shall preserve you of His bounty if He will. Lo! Allah is Knower, Wise.

IX/73 : Oh Prophet! Strive against the disbelievers and the hypocrites! Be harsh with them. Their ultimate abode is hell, a hapless journey's-end.

XCVIII/6 : Lo! those who disbelieve, among the People of the Scripture and the idolaters, will abide in fire of hell. They are the worst of created beings.

X/5 : Unto Him is the return of all of you; it is a promise of Allah in truth. Lo! He produceth creation, then reproduceth it, that He may reward those who believe and do good works with equity; while, as for those who disbelieve, theirs will be a boiling drink and painful doom because they disbelieved.

LXIX/30-37 : (It will be said): Take him and fetter him
And then expose him to hell-fire
And then insert him in a chain whereof the length is seventy cubits.
Lo! he used not to believe in Allah the Tremendous,
And urged not on the feeding of the wretched,
Therefor hath he no lover here this day,
Nor any food save filth
Which none but sinners eat.

LXVIII/14-16 : It is because he is possessed of wealth and children
That, when Our revelations are recited unto him, he saith: Mere fables of the men of old.
We shall brand him on the nose.

LXVII/6 : And for those who disbelieve in their Lord there is the doom of hell, a hapless journey's end!

XLVII/12 : Lo! Allah will cause those who believe and do good works to enter Gardens underneath which rivers flow; while those who disbelieve take their comfort in this life and eat even as the cattle eat, and the Fire is their habitation.

XLIV/43-50 : Lo! the tree of Zaqqum[2] ,
The food of the sinner!
Like molten brass, it seetheth in their bellies
As the seething of boiling water.
(And it will be said): Take him and drag him to the midst of hell,
Then pour upon his head the torment of boiling water.
(Saying): Taste! Lo! thou wast forsooth the mighty, the noble!
Lo! this is that whereof ye used to doubt.

XXXVII/67-68 : And afterward, lo! thereupon they have a drink of boiling water
And afterward, lo! their return is surely unto hell.

V/33-34 : The only reward of those who make war upon Allah and His messenger and strive after corruption in the land will be that they will be killed or crucified, or have their hands and feet on alternate sides cut off, or will be expelled out of the land. Such will be their degradation in the world, and in the Hereafter theirs will be an awful doom;
Save those who repent before ye overpower them. For know that Allah is Forgiving, Merciful.

V/72-73 : They surely disbelieve who say: Lo! Allah is the Messiah, son of Mary. The Messiah (himself) said: O Children of Israel, worship Allah, my Lord and your Lord. Lo!

whoso ascribeth partners unto Allah, for him Allah hath forbidden Paradise. His abode is the Fire. For evil-doers there will be no helpers.
They surely disbelieve who say: Lo! Allah is the third of three; when there is no God save the One God. If they desist not from so saying a painful doom will fall on those of them who disbelieve.

XXII/19-22 : These twain (the believers and the disbelievers) are two opponents who contend concerning their Lord. But as for those who disbelieve, garments of fire will be cut out for them; boiling fluid will be poured down on their heads.
Whereby that which is in their bellies, and their skins too, will be melted;
And for them are hooked rods of iron.
Whenever, in their anguish, they would go forth from thence they are driven back therein and (it is said unto them): Taste the doom of burning.

LXXVI/4 : Lo! We have prepared for disbelievers manacles and carcans and a raging fire.

Footnotes

1. N.J. Dawood translates in his 'The Koran': 'Strike off their heads, maim them in every limb!'

2. Zaqqum tree: a tree that grows in the heart of hell bearing fruit like devils' heads.

CHAPTER 3

THE KORAN'S PROMISES

The Koran promises many desirable rewards for the Moslems in Allah's heaven.

LXXVI/13-22 : Reclining therein upon couches, they will find there neither (heat of) a sun nor bitter cold. The shade thereof is close upon them and the clustered fruits thereof bow down. Goblets of silver are brought round for them, and beakers (as) of glass (Bright as) glass but (made) of silver, which they (themselves) have measured to the measure (of their deeds). There are they watered with a cup whereof the mixture is of Zanjabil, The water of a spring therein, named Salsabil. There serve them youths of everlasting youth, whom, when thou seest, thou wouldst take for scattered pearls. When thou seest, thou wilt see there bliss and high estate. Their raiment will be fine green silk and gold embroidery. Bracelets of silver will they wear. Their Lord will slake their thirst with a pure drink. (And it will be said unto them): Lo! this is a reward for you. Your endeavor (upon earth) hath found acceptance.

LV/46-59 : But for him who feareth the standing before his Lord there are two gardens.

Which is it, of the favors of your Lord, that
ye deny?
Of spreading branches.
Which is it, of the favors of your Lord, that
ye deny?
Wherein are two fountains flowing.
Which is it, of the favors of your Lord, that
ye deny?
Wherein is every kind of fruit in pairs.
Which is it, of the favors of your Lord, that
ye deny?
Reclining upon couches lined with silk bro-
cade, the fruit of both gardens near to
hand.
Which is it, of the favors of your Lord, that
ye deny?
Therein are those of modest gaze[1] ,whom
neither man nor jinni will have touched
before them,
Which is it, of the favors of your Lord, that
ye deny?
(In beauty) like the jacynth and the coral
stone.
Which is it, of the favors of your Lord, that
ye deny?

LXXXIII/22-28 : Lo! the righteous verily are in delight,
On couches, gazing.
Thou wilt know in their faces the radiance
of delight.
They are given to drink of a pure wine,
sealed,
Whose seal is musk - For this let (all) those
strive who strive for bliss -
And mixed with water of Tasnim,
A spring whence those brought near to
Allah drink.

LVI/35-40 : Lo! We have created them a (new) creation
And made them virgins,
Lovers, friends,
For those on the right hand;

A multitude of those old
And a multitude of those of later time.

LVI/11-24   : Those are they who will be brought nigh
In gardens of delight;
A multitude of those of old
And a few of those of later time,
On lined couches,
Reclining therein face to face.
There wait on them immortal youths
With bowls and ewers and a cup from a
pure spring
Wherefrom they get no aching of the head
nor any madness,
And fruit that they prefer
And flesh of fowls that they desire.
And (there are) fair ones with wide, lovely
eyes,
Like unto hidden pearls,
Reward for what they used to do.

Footnote

1.   ..those of modest gaze is translated as 'bashful virgins'
by Dr N.J. Dawood in the Holy Koran translated by him.

CHAPTER 4

A MOSLEM'S CONDUCT

The Koran advises the believers on the subject of infidels in their neighborhoods and circles of friends.

IX/123 : O ye who believe! Fight those of the disbelievers who are near to you, and let them find harshness in you, and know that Allah is with those who keep their duty (unto Him).

IV/144 : O ye who believe! Choose not disbelievers for (your) friends in place of believers. Would you give Allah a clear warrant against you?

V/51 : O ye who believe! Take not the Jews and Christians for friends. They are friends one to another. He among you who taketh them for friends is (one) of them. Lo! Allah guideth not wrongdoing folk.

III/118 : O ye who believe! Take not for intimates others than your own folk, who would spare no pains to ruin you; they love to hamper you. Hatred is revealed by (the utterance of) their mouths, but that which their breasts hide is greater. We have made plain for you the revelations if ye will understand.

IX/122 : And the believers should not all go out to fight. Of every troop of them, a party only should go forth, that they (who are left behind) may gain sound knowledge in religion, and that they may warn their folk

12

when they return to them, so that they may beware.

IV/160-161 : Because of the wrongdoing of the Jews We forbade them good things which were (before) made lawful unto them, and because of their much hindering from Allah's way, And of their taking usury when they were forbidden it and of their devouring people's wealth by false pretenses. We have prepared for those of them who disbelieve a painful doom.

VI/147 : Unto those who are Jews We forbade every animal with claws. And of the oxen and the sheep forbade We unto them the fat thereof save that upon the backs or the entrails, or that which is mixed with the bone. That We awarded them for their rebellion. And lo! We verily are Truthful.

V/57 : O ye who believe! Choose not for friends such of those who received the Scripture before you, and of the disbelievers, as make a jest and sport of your religion. But keep your duty to Allah if ye are true believers.

IV/101 : And when ye go forth in the land, it is no sin for you to curtail (your) worship if ye fear that those who disbelieve may attack you. In truth the disbelievers are an open enemy to you.

IV/102 : And when thou (O Muhammad) art among them and arrangest (their) worship for them, let only a party of them stand with thee (to worship) and let them take their arms. Then when they have performed their prostrations let them fall to the rear and let another party come that hath not worshipped and let them worship with thee, and let them take their precaution and their arms. Those who disbelieve long for you to neglect your arms and your baggage that they may attack you once for all. It is no sin for you to lay aside your arms, if rain impedeth you or ye are sick. But take your precaution. Lo! Allah prepareth for the disbelievers shameful punishment.

CHAPTER 5

THE KORAN'S WARNINGS

The Koran spells out stern warnings to nations of disbelievers. The threats and warnings are a reminder that Allah is all-powerful.

L/36 : And how many a generation We destroyed before them, who were mightier than these in prowess so that they overran the lands! Had they any place of refuge (when the judgement came)?

VII/97-99 : Are the people of the townships then secure from the coming of Our wrath upon them as a night-raid while they sleep? Or are the people of the townships then secure from the coming of Our wrath upon them in the daytime while they play? Are they then secure from Allah's scheme? None deemeth himself secure from Allah's scheme save folk that perish.

XXII/45 : How many a township have We destroyed while it was sinful, so that it lieth (to this day) in ruins, and (how many) a deserted well and lofty tower!

XXII/48 : And how many a township did I suffer long though it was sinful! Then I grasped it. Unto Me is the return.

VI/6 : See they not how many a generation We destroyed before them, whom We had established in the earth more firmly than We have established you, and We shed on them abundant showers from the sky, and made the rivers flow beneath them. Yet We destroyed them for their sins, and created after them another generation.

CHAPTER 6

THE KORAN ON LOOT OR SPOIL

The Koran's injunctions on looted property which includes women and children and those men that for some reason
or other were not killed in raids and were taken as captives.
Such men, women and children were classed as slaves. The
slaves were merchandise that could be sold, maltreated or
killed without compunction with or without valid reason, by
the believer.

LIX/5-6 : Whatsoever palm-trees ye cut down or left
standing on their roots, it was by Allah's
leave, in order that He might confound the
evil-livers.
And that which Allah gave as spoil unto His
messenger from them, ye urged not any
horse or riding-camel for the sake thereof,
but Allah giveth His messenger lordship
over whom He will. Allah is Able to do all
things.

XLIX/20-21 : Allah promiseth you much booty that ye
will capture, and hath given you this in
advance, and hath withheld men's hands
from you, that it may be a token for the
believers, and that He may guide you on a
right path.
And other (gain), which ye have not been
able to achieve, Allah will compass it.
Allah is Able to do all things.

VIII/41 : And know that whatever ye take as spoils
of war, lo! a fifth thereof is for Allah, and
for the messenger and for the kinsman

17

(who hath need) and orphans and the needy and the wayfarer, if ye believe in Allah and that which We revealed unto Our slave on the Day of Discrimination, the day when the two armies met.
And Allah is Able to do all things.

VIII/65 : O Prophet! Exhort the believers to fight. If there be of you twenty stedfast they shall overcome two hundred, and if there be of you a hundred stedfast they shall overcome a thousand of those who disbelieve, because they (the disbelievers) are a folk without intelligence.

VIII/67-69 : It is not for any Prophet to have captives until he hath made slaughter in the land. Ye desire the lure of this world and Allah desireth (for you) the Hereafter, and Allah is Mighty, Wise.
Had it not been for an ordinance of Allah which had gone before, an awful doom had come upon you on account of what ye took. Now enjoy what ye have won, as lawful and good, and keep your duty to Allah. Lo! Allah is Forgiving, Merciful .

VIII/73 : And those who disbelieve are protectors one of another.
- If ye do not so, there will be confusion in the land, and great corruption.

Footnotes

1. vv. 67-69 were revealed when the Prophet had decided to spare the lives of the prisoners taken at Badr and hold them to ranson, against the wish of Umar, who would have executed them for their past crimes. The Prophet took the verses as a reproof, and they are generally understood to mean that no quarter ought to have been given in that first battle.

CHAPTER 7

THE KORAN AND MOSLEM WOMEN

The principal injunctions of the Koran on Moslem women are as follows:

II/223   : Your women are a tilth for you (to culti-
                  vate) so go to your tilth as ye will, and
                  send (good deeds) before you for your souls,
                  and fear Allah, and know that ye will (one
                  day) meet Him. Give glad tidings to be-
                  lievers, O Muhammad).

IV/23   : Forbidden unto you are your mothers, and
                  your daughters, and your sisters, and your
                  father's sisters, and your mother's sisters,
                  and your brother's daughters and your sis-
                  ter's daughters, and your foster-mothers,
                  and your foster-sisters, and your mothers-
                  in-law, and your step-daughters who are
                  under your protection (born) of your women
                  unto whom ye have gone in - but if ye have
                  not gone in unto them, then it is no sin for
                  you (to marry their daughters) - and the
                  wives of your sons who (spring) from your
                  own loins. And (it is forbidden unto you)
                  that ye should have two sisters together,
                  except what hath already happened (of that
                  nature) in the past. Lo! Allah is ever
                  Forgiving, Merciful.

IV/15   : As for those of your women who are guilty
                  of lewdness, call to witness four of you
                  against them. And if they testify (to the
                  truth of the allegation) then confine them

to the houses until death take them or (until) Allah appoint for them a way (through new legislation).

II/230 : And if he hath divorced her (the third time), then she is not lawful unto him thereafter until she hath wedded another husband. Then if he (the other husband) divorce her it is no sin for both of them that they come together again if they consider that they are able to observe the limits of Allah. These are the limits of Allah. He manifesteth them for people who have knowledge.

II/221 : Wed not idolatresses till they believe; for lo! a believeing bondwoman is better than an idolatress though she please you; and give not your daughters in marriage to idolaters till they believe, for lo! a believing slave is better than an idolater though he please you. These invite unto the Fire, and Allah inviteth unto the Garden, and unto forgiveness by His grace, and expoundeth thus His revelations to mankind that haply they may remember.

IV/34 : Men are in charge of women, because Allah hath made the one of them to excel the other, and because they spend of their property (for the support of women). So good women are the obedient, guarding in secret that which Allah hath guarded. As for those from whom ye fear rebellion, admonish them and banish them to beds apart, and scourge[1] them. Then if they obey you, seek not a way against them. Lo! Allah is ever High Exalted, Great.

XXIII/1-11 : Successful indeed are the believers
Who are humble in their prayers,
And who shun vain conversation,
And who are payers of the poor-due;

And who guard their modesty -
Save from their wives or the (slaves) that
their right[2] hands possess, for then they are
not blameworthy,
But whoso craveth beyond that, such are
transgressors -
And who are shepherds of their pledge and
their covenant,
And who pay heed to their prayers.
These are the heirs
Who will inherit Paradise. There they will
abide.

XXIV/6-7   : As for those who accuse their wives but
have no witnesses except themselves; let
the testimony of one of them be four testi-
monies, (swearing) by Allah that he is of
those who speak the truth;
And yet a fifth, invoking the curse of Allah
on him if he is of those who lie.

XXIV/60   : As for women past child-bearing, who have
no hope of marriage, it is no sin for them if
they discard their (outer) clothing in such a
way as not to show adornment but to
refrain is better for them. Allah is Hearer,
Knower.

LX/10   : O ye who believe! When believing women
come unto you as fugitives, examine them.
Allah is best aware of their faith. Then, if
ye know them for true believers, send them
not back unto the disbelievers. They are
not lawful for the disbelievers, nor are the
disbelievers lawful for them. And give the
disbelivers that which they have spent
(upon them). And it is no sin for you to
marry such women when ye have given
them their dues. And hold not to the ties
of disbelieving women; and ask for (the
return of) that which ye have spent; and let
the disbelievers ask for that which they
have spent. That is the judgement of
Allah. He judgeth between you. Allah is
Knower, Wise.

Note: Ghazzali, the renowned Islamic thinker had summed the eighteen pains that had been visited on Moslem women as a punishment of Eve's transgression in Paradise. The list eloquently shows the position of women in Islam and how the social customs were backed up by the prophet's religion.

They are: menstruation, childbirth, separation from parents to get married to a stranger, pregnancy, not having control over her own person, smaller share in inheritance, liability to get divorced and inability to divorce herself, having only one husband at a time while the husband can have four wives at the same time not counting the concubines, having to keep her head covered within the four walls, having to stay secluded within the four walls, her testimony having only half the strength of a man's testimony, not being able to go out alone but only when accompanied by a near relative, not being able to take part in Friday and festive day prayers and at funerals, not being able to serve as a judge or ruler, having to wait four months and ten days after the death of a husband before remarrying [3] , having to wait three months after getting divorced by a husband before remarrying, having very little merit when compared to men and having half the sentence of punishment for profligacy [4] when compared to that of a man.

Footnotes

1. N.J. Dawood's Koran tanslates 'scourge' as 'beat'.

2. 'right hand' signifies 'won in battle by force of arms'.

3. the waiting period is to ensure that the woman does not carry the child of the dead husband or the husband that divorced her.

4. this punishment is really a relief instead of a 'pain'.

CHAPTER 8

THE KORAN ON FOOD, ALMS AND OTHER THINGS

V/3 : Forbidden unto you (for food) are carrion and blood and swine-flesh, and that which hath been dedicated unto any other than Allah, and the strangled, and the dead through beating, and the dead through falling from a height, and that which hath been killed by (the goring of) horns, and the devoured of wild beasts, saving that which ye make lawful (by the death stroke), and that which hath been immolated unto idols. And (forbidden is it) that ye swear by the divining arrows. This is an abomination. This day are those who disbelieve in despair of (ever harming) your religion; so fear them not, fear Me! This day have I perfected your religion for you and completed My favor unto you, and have chosen for you as religion AL ISLAM[1] . Whoso is forced by hunger, not by will, to sin: (for him) lo! Allah is Forgiving, Merciful[2] .

IX/60 : The alms are only for the poor and the needy, and those who collect them, and those whose hearts are to be reconciled[3] , and to free the captives and the debtors, and for the cause of Allah, and (for) the wayfarers; a duty imposed by Allah. Allah is Knower, Wise.

XXIX/8 : We have enjoined on man kindness to parents; but if they strive to make thee join with Me that of which thou hast no

23

knowledge, then obey them not. Unto Me is your return and I shall tell you what ye used to do[4].

IV/43   : O ye who believe! Draw not near unto your prayer when ye are drunken, till ye know that which ye utter, nor when ye are polluted, save when journeying upon the road, till ye have bathed. And if ye be ill, or on a journey, or one of you cometh from the closet, or ye have touched women[5] , and ye find not water, then go to high clean soil and rub your faces and your hands (therewith). Lo! Allah is Benign, Forgiving.

Footnotes

1. AL ISLAM is surrender to Allah.

2. If forced by hunger a Moslem is allowed to eat food which is normally forbidden.

3. 'Reconciled' here means 'conversion' to Islam.

4. In other words, 'do not obey your parents' if they are non-Moslems.

5. N.J. Dawood translates 'touched women' as 'had intercourse with women' in his Koran.

Note: It is not quite clear how a Moslem, who by definition does not take intoxicating drinks, can get drunk. 'Touched women' or what N.J. Dawood calls 'had intercourse with women' mean had sex with one's own married women or slave-girls owned by the believer. Intercourse with unwed women or women wedded to other believers is forbidden. Kafir women are to be treated as slave-girls. However, temporary marriages, also called Muta' marriages, lasting for a few hours to a few years and ending at a previously stipulated time, are allowed in Islam.

Islam forbids prostitution.

CHAPTER 9

ISLAM IN ACTION I

It was around 627 A.D. that prophet Mohammed raided the Jewish tribe of Qurayza. The Jews were defeated in the fight and many prisoners were taken. They were either sold or assassinated. In one place alone some 800 Jews were beheaded in cold blood. One Jew was let go as he renounced his ancestral religion and accepted Islam. In the year 629 A.D. after the battle of Khaybar and the defeat of the Jews the same play was enacted. All the Jews were put to the sword. The raids undertaken by the prophet and the methods followed became the guide-lines for the caliphs that followed him. The blood that flowed in Persia when caliph Umar conquered that land still horrifies the present-day Iranians. To indicate their happiness at the demise of Umar, Iranians dress themselves up in festive clothing on the death anniversary of this caliph, even to this day.

a)   THE PATTERN

The thoughts and deeds of prophet Mohammed and his caliphs became the honorable examples to be followed by all Moslems in later years. In his famous book 'Story of Civilisation' Will Durant has written that "the Mohammedan conquest of India was probably the bloodiest story in history". The magnitude of crimes credited to Moslem monarchs by the medieval Moslem historians is beyond measure. What strikes as significant is the broad pattern of those crimes. The pattern is that of a 'jihad' (holy war) against the infidels in which the 'ghazis' (religious warriors and conquerors) of Islam undertake 'ghazzuas' or raids in order to

1 invade the lands of the infidels;

2 massacre as many infidel men, women and children as they like after winning a victory;

3 capture the survivors to be sold as slaves and some retained in their harems as slave-girls;

4 plunder every place and person for war booty, a fifth of which (including the slaves) went to the caliph or some other religious head;

5 demolish the places of worship of the infidels and build mosques in their places; and

6 defile and desecrate the deities and other symbols of the infidels' religions by throwing them into public squares or making into steps leading to the prayer area of the believers.

What is still more significant is that this is exactly the pattern

1 revealed by Allah in the Koran;

2 practised, perfected and prescribed by the prophet in his own life-time and meticulously followed by the caliphs that followed;

3 elaborated in the Hadis (the other religious book of Islam) with great attention to detail;

4 certified by the mullahs in all ages including our own; and

5 followed by all Moslem kings and leaders who aspired after name and fame in this life and houris hereafter.

b)   ALEXANDRIA, VISALDEVA, NALANDA, DACCA

When the conquering Moslem invaders arrived in Alexandria and stood in front of the famous library there, the Moslem general did not know if he should destroy such a renowned store-house of knowledge. He sent his horseman to caliph Umar for his instructions. The caliph replied: "If these writings of the Greeks agree with the book of Allah, they are useless and need not be preserved: if they disagree, they are pernicious and ought to be destroyed". There was thus only one fate for the infidels' seat of learning. The library of the Ptolemies was thus burnt down and the episode settled for all time, in the minds of the Moslems, the method of dealing with libraries, universities, schools and colleges, which had nothing to do with warfare, but belonged to the infidels.

Thus the capital of Gujarat was attacked by Qutbuddin Aibak in the year 1196 A.D. and the famous Sanskrit College of Visaldeva was destroyed and a mosque known as 'adhai din ka jhompada' was built on the same foundations. The famous Buddhist University of Nalanda had the same fate, in the year 1200 A.D. when Muhammad Bakhtyar Khalji attacked the township and massacred the harmless Buddhist monks and violated the nuns.   When, in recent years, the Pakistani Moslem army attacked the then East Pakistan (now Bangladesh), the first attack was launched on Dacca University. Even the women students were not spared. They were raped and then murdered.

c)   NO CODE OF HONOR IN ISLAM

India before the advent of Islamic imperialism was not exactly a zone of peace. There were plenty of wars fought by Hindu kings. But in all their wars certain time-honored conventions were observed by the warring factions. The priests and monks were never molested.   The houses of worship were never touched. The chastity of women was never violated. The non-combatants were never killed or captured. A human habitation was never attacked unless it was a fort.   The civil population was never plundered. War booty was an unknown item in the calculations of a conqueror. The martial classes who clashed, mostly in open spaces, had a code of honor.

Sacrifice of honor for victory or material gain was deemed as worse than death.

Islamic imperialism knew no code of honor. The only rule of war they observed without fail was to fall upon the helpless civil population after a decisive victory had been won on the battlefield. They sacked and burnt down villages and towns after the defenders had died fighting or had fled. The priests, monks and nuns invited their special attention in a mass-murder of non-combatants. The houses of worship were their special targets in an orgy of pillage and destruction. Those whom they did not kill, they captured and sold as slaves. WOMEN WERE THEIR PRIZE; THEY SEIZED THEM TO VIO-LATE THEM AND CARRY THEM AWAY WITH THEM AS BONDED SLAVES INTO THEIR HAREMS. As late as in 1971, the Moslem army of Pakistan killed thousands of young women, mostly Hindus or infidels in their language. The most attractive among them were held to become sex-slaves in the military cantonments. When a few of the girls attempted to hang themselves with their saris or clothing, their garments were taken away from them and held in captivity stark naked. And these were the followers of the 'ghazis' in the service of Allah and Islam.

The Hindus found it very hard to understand the psychology of this new invader. For the first time in their history, the Hindus were witnessing, as their counterparts, the Christians did at the outset of Islamic invasion of Europe, a scene that went beyond their imagination. One historian wrote: "The conquering army burnt villages, devastated the land, plundered people's wealth, took priests and children and women of all classes captive, flogged with thongs of raw hide, carried a moving prison with it, and converted the prisoners into obsequious Turks."

d)   MAHMUD OF GHAZNI

Utbi, the historian at the time of Mahmud of Ghazni wrote about one such raid by the Moslem invader: "The Sultan returned in the rear of an immense booty, and slaves were so plentiful that they became very cheap and men of respectability in their native land were degraded by becoming slaves of common shopkeepers in Moslem lands. BUT THIS IS THE GOODNESS OF ALLAH, WHO BESTOWS HONOR ON HIS OWN RELIGION AND DEGRADES INFIDELITY."

e)   MOHAMMED GHORI

Mohammed Ghori attacked the Hindus several times and after each attack a general massacre followed. Rapes and pillage came afterward. The Gahadvad treasuries at Asni and Varanasi were plundered. Moslem historian Hasan Nizami rejoices that "in Benares which is the center of the country of Hind (India), they destroyed one thousand temples and raised mosques on their foundations." According to Kamilut-Tawarikh of Ibn Asr, "the slaughter of Hindus at Varanasi was immense; none were spared except women and children, and the carnage of men went on until the earth was weary."

f)   FIRUZ TUGHLAK

Firuz Tughlak attacked Orissa in 1360 A.D. and destroyed the temple of Jagannath. After the sack of the temple, he attacked an island on the sea-coast where "nearly 100,000 men of Jajnagar had taken refuge with their women, children and kinsmen". The swordsmen of Islam turned 'the island into a basin of blood by the massacre of the unbelievers'. A worse fate overtook the Hindu women. Sirat-i-Firuz Shahi records" "WOMEN WITH BABIES AND PREGNANT LADIES WERE HALTERED, MANACLED, FETTERED AND CHAINED, AND PRESSED AS SLAVES INTO SERVICE IN THE HOUSE OF EVERY SOLDIER".'

g)   TIMUR

Then came Timur the Terrible. Timur, in his Tuzk-i-Taimuri starts by saying: "O Prophet, make war upon the infidels and unbelievers, and treat them severely. My great object in invading Hindusthan had been to wage a religious war against the infidel Hindus. . .the army of Islam might gain something by plundering the wealth and valuables of the Hindus."

To start with he stormed the fort of Kator on the border of Kashmir. He ordered the soldiers "to kill all the men, to make prisoners of women and children, and to plunder and lay waste all their property." NEXT HE "DIRECTED TOWERS TO BE BUILT ON THE MOUNTAIN OF THE SKULLS OF THOSE OBSTINATE UNBELIEVERS."

Soon after he laid siege to Bhatnir defended by the Rajputs. They surrendered after some fight and were pardoned. But Islam did not bind Timur to keep his word given to the "unbelievers", His Tuzk-i-Taimuri records: "In a short space of time all the people in the fort were put to the sword, and in the course of one hour the heads of 10,000 infidels were cut off. The sword of Islam was washed in the blood of the infidels, and all the goods and effects, the treasure and the grain which for many a long year had been stored in the fort became the spoils of my soldiers. They set fire to the houses and reduced them to ashes, and they razed the buildings and the fort to the ground."

At Sarsuti, the next city to be sacked, "all these infidel Hindus were slain, their wives and children were made prisoners and their property and goods became the spoils of the victors." Timur was now moving through the land of the Jats, a martial people. He directed his soldiers to "plunder and destroy and kill everyone whom they met". "And so the soldiers plundered every village, killed the men, and carried a number of Hindu prisoners, both male and female."

Loni, which he captured before he arrived at Delhi was predominantly a Hindu town. But some Moslem inhabitants were also taken prisoner. TIMUR ORDERED THAT "THE MUSULMAN PRISONERS SHOULD BE SEPARATED AND SAVED, BUT THE INFIDELS SHOULD ALL BE DESPATCHED TO HELL WITH THE PROSELYTISING SWORD".

By now Timur had captured 100,000 Hindus. As he prepared for battle against the Tughlak army after crossing the Jumna river, his advisers told him that on the great day of battle these 100,000 Hindu prisoners could not be left unattended and that it would be opposed to the rules of war to set these idolators and enemies of Islam at liberty. ONE HUNDRED

THOUSAND UNARMED HINDU PRISONERS WERE SLAUGH-
TERED FORTHWITH[1].

Then came the sack of Delhi. Tuzk-i-Taimuri concludes:
"Many of the Hindus drew their swords and resisted... The
flames of strife were thus lighted and spread through the
whole city from Jahanpanah and Siri to Old Delhi, burning up
all it reached. The Hindus set fire to their houses with their
own hands, burned their women and children in them and
rushed to fight and were killed...On that day, Thursday, and
all night of Friday, nearly 15,000 Turks were engaged in
slaying, plundering and destroying. When morning broke on
Friday, all my army...went off to the city and thought of
nothing but killing, plundering and making prisoners...The
following day, Saturday the 17th, all passed the same way, and
the spoil was so great that each man secured from fifty to a
hundred prisoners, men, women and children. There was no
man who took less than twenty. The other booty was immense
in rubies, diamonds, garnets, pearls and other gems and jewels.
Gold and silver ornaments of Hindu women were obtained in
such quantities as to exceed all account. EXCEPTING THE
QUARTER OF THE MULLAHS AND SOME AREAS WHERE
OTHER MOSLEMS LIVED, THE ENTIRE CITY OF DELHI WAS
SACKED."

h)   MUZAFFAR SHAH

IN 1391 A.D. THE MOSLEMS OF GUJARAT COMPLAINED TO
NASIRUDDIN MUHAMMAD, THE TUGHLAK SULTAN OF
DELHI, THAT THE LOCAL GOVERNOR, FARHAT-UL-MULK,
WAS PRACTISING TOLERANCE TOWARD THE HINDUS OF
GUJARAT. The sultan immediately appointed Muzaffar Khan
as the new governor sending Farhat-ul-Mulk away. Soon the
sultan of Delhi died and Muzaffar Khan declared himself an
independent king and took the name of Muzaffar Shah. In 1393
A.D. he led an expedition to destroy the famous temple of
Somnath which had been rebuilt by the Hindus after the pillage
by Mahmud of Ghazni. Muzaffar Shah killed many Hindus on
that occasion to 'chastise' them for having had the 'impudence'
of rebuilding a temple that had been destroyed and desecrated
by a servant of Allah. He raised a mosque on top of the
foundation of the destroyed temple. The Hindus however

restarted restoring the temple. In 1401 A.D. the iconoclast sultan came back with a huge army and once again killed a great number of Hindus and rebuilt another mosque at the same place.

i)   MAHMUD BEGARHA

Mahmud Begarha who became the sultan of Gujarat in 1458 A.D. was the worst fanatic of this dynasty. One of his vassals was the chieftain of Junagadh who had never withheld the regular tribute to the sultan. Yet in 1469 A.D. Mahmud invaded Junagadh. IN REPLY TO THE CHIEFTAIN'S PRO-TESTS, MAHMUD SAID THAT HE WAS NOT INTERESTED IN MONEY AS MUCH AS IN THE SPREAD OF ISLAM. THE CHIEFTAIN WHO WAS A HINDU WAS FORCIBLY CON-VERTED TO ISLAM AND JUNAGADH WAS RENAMED MUSTAFABAD. In 1472 A.D. Mahmud attacked Dwaraka, destroyed the Krishna temple and plundered the city. Jaysingh, the ruler of Champaner and his minister were murdered by Mahmud for refusing to accept Islam after they had been defeated and their country pillaged and plundered. Champaner was renamed Mahmudabad.

j)   MAHMUD KHALJI

Mahmud Khalji of Malwa (1436-69 A.D.) also destroyed Hindu temples and revelled in building mosques at the same place. He heaped many insults on the Hindus.

k)   ILYAS SHAH

Ilyas Shah of Bengal (1339-79 A.D.) invaded Nepal and destroy-ed the temple of Swayambhunath at Kathmandu. He also invaded Orissa and demolished many temples and plundered at many places. THE BAHMANI SULTANS OF GULBARGA AND BIDAR CONSIDERED IT THEIR SACRED DUTY TO KILL A HUNDRED THOUSAND MEN, WOMEN AND CHILDREN EVERY YEAR. They demolished and desecrated Hindu tem-ples all over South India.

l) BABUR

The scene shifted once more to Delhi after Babur came out victorious against the Lodhis and the Rajputs. The founder of the great Mughal empire has received much acclaim for his fortitude in adversity, his daring against heavy odds, his swimming prowess, his love of flowers and pomegranates, and so on and so forth. But his face, presented by himself in his Tuzk-i-Baburi, suffers an irreparable damage if denuded of the rich hues of horrible cruelties in which he habitually indulged.

The lurid details he provides of his repeated massacres of the 'infidels' leave no doubt that he was very proud of his performance. He was particularly fond of raising higher and higher towers of Hindu heads cut off during and after every battle he fought with them. He loved to sit in his royal tent to watch this 'spectacle'. The prisoners were brought before him and butchered by his 'brave' swordsmen. ON ONE OCCASION THE GROUND FLOWED WITH SO MUCH BLOOD AND BE-CAME SO FULL OF QUIVERING CARCASSES THAT HIS TENT HAD TO BE REMOVED THRICE TO A HIGHER LEVEL. He lost no opportunity of capturing prisoners of war and amassing the booty. He only missed the merit of demolishing temples and breaking images because his predecessors Firuz Tughlak and others had hardly left any for him in the areas he traversed. In the dynasty founded by him, it was incumbent that every king should style himself a 'ghazi', that is a warrior for Islam who took part in 'ghazzua' or raids on infidels or kafirs.

m) SHER SHAH SURI

Sher Shah Suri's name is associated with the Grand Trunk Road of North India, extending from Peshawar to Dacca, with caravanserais and several other schemes of public welfare. It is true that he was not a habitual persecutor of the Hindus. But he did not betray Islam when the test came at Raisen in 1543 A.D. Shaikh Nurul Haq records in Zubadatul-Tawarikh as follows: "In the year 950 Hijri, Puranmal, a Hindu chieftain, held occupation of the fort of Raisen. . .He had 1000 women in his entourage and amongst them several Moslem women. Sher Khan's Moslem pride was offended and the servant of Allah resolved to attack the fort. After he had been engaged in investing the fort for some time, an accommodation was proposed. It was finally agreed that Puranmal will be allowed safe conduct along with his family and children as well as 4000 Rajputs.

SEVERAL MULLAHS GAVE HIM THE OPINION THAT ISLAM DICTATES THAT THESE INFIDELS SHOULD ALL BE KILLED NOTWITHSTANDING THE AGREEMENT, FOR A MOSLEM IS NOT BOUND BY ANY AGREEMENT MADE WITH AN INFIDEL. Consequently, the whole army was brought and placed in position to attack the Rajputs when they were the most vulnerable. They were all killed to a man.

n)   AKBAR THE GREAT

Humayun, the son of Babur and father of Akbar had hardly any time free from troubles to devote in the service of Islam and 'kafir-kushi'[2] (killing of infidels). But his son Akbar made quite a good start as a 'ghazi'. He struck the half-dead Hindu king Himu with his sword after the second battle of Panipat. The ritual was then followed by many more 'brave warriors' of Islam led by Bairam Khan who stuck their swords in the dead body. In 1568 A.D. Akbar ordered a general massacre at Chitor, Rajputana after the fort had fallen. Abul Fazl records in Akbar-nama as follows: "There were 8,000 fighting Rajputs collected in the fortress, but there were more than 40,000 peasants who took part in watching and serving.

From early dawn till midday the bodies of those ill-starred men were consumed by the majesty of the great warrior. Nearly 30,000 men were killed. . . when Sultan Alauddin Khalji took the fort after a siege of six months and seven days, the peasantry were not put to death as they had not engaged in fighting. But on this occasion orders were given for general massacre. Akbar thus improved upon the record of Alauddin Khalji. WATCHING AND SERVING WERE REINTERPRETED AS ACTS OF WAR.

o)   JAHANGIR

Jahangir was too indolent to keep his promise, given to Nawab Murtaza Khan at the time of accession to the throne, that he would uphold the laws of Islam or Shariat. He was just too much devoted to the wine-cup and women of his harem and did not care so much for Islam in his private life. But he encouraged conversion to Islam by offering daily allowances to those who renounced their ancestral faith and accepted the Moslem creed.

In the eighth year of his reign he destroyed the temple of Bhagwat at Ajmer. He persecuted the Jains of Gujarat. He tortured to death the Sikh holy man and leader Guru Arjun Dev. Guru Arjun Dev was murdered in a terrible way. THE GURU WAS MADE TO SIT BY FORCE ON A HOT STEEL PLATE WHICH HAD A BIG FIRE UNDERNEATH. HE WAS THEN COVERED WITH HOT SAND POURED FROM OVER HIS HEAD. AND TO INSULT HIM FURTHER, HIS BODY WAS WRAPPED WITH THE SKIN OF A FRESHLY SLAUGHTERED COW. The manner of assassination resembles what the Koran advises for killing the infidels.

The fault of the Sikh Guru was that he had refused to give up his own religion for Islam and to include some verses from the Koran in the Sikh holy book, the Granth Sahib.

p)   SHAH JAHAN

The pendulum started to swing toward the true spirit of Islam at the very start of Shah Jahan's reign in 1623 A.D. Its outer symbol was the reappearance of the beard on the face of the emperor. Abdul Hamid Lahori records in his badshah-nama: "It had been brought to the notice of the Emperor that during the last reign, construction of many Hindu temples had been started, but remained still unfinished in Benares, the holy city of the Hindus, the infidels. The temples were now to be completed. The emperor issued orders to destroy all temples of Benares as well as elsewhere in his domain, before they were finished. It was reported from the province of Allahabad that 76 Hindu temples had been destroyed in Benares alone." The year was 1633 A.D.

At the beginning of his reign, the people of Kashmir, both Hindus and Moslems used to live amicably. They used to intermarry, and the wife, whatever might have been her father's faith, accepted the faith of the husband. In October, 1634 A.D., Shah Jahan forbade the custom and ordered that every Hindu who had taken a Moslem wife must either embrace Islam and be married anew to his wife, or he must give her up to be wedded to a Moslem. The order was rigorously enforced.

In 1635 A.D. Shah Jahan's soldiers captured some ladies of the royal Bundela family after Jujhar Singh and his sons failed to kill them in the time-honored Rajput tradition to avoid falling into the hands of the enemy. In the words of Sir Jadu Nath Sarkar, the eminent historian: "A terrible fate awaited the captive ladies who survived; mothers and daughters of kings, they were robbed of their religion, and forced to lead the infamous life of the Mughal harem - to be the unloved plaything of their master's passions for a day or two and then doomed to sigh out their days like bondwomen, without knowing the dignity of a wife or the joys of a mother. SWEETER FAR FOR THEM WOULD HAVE BEEN DEATH FROM THE HANDS OF THEIR DEAR ONES THAN SUBMISSION TO A RACE THAT KNEW NO GENEROSITY TO THE FALLEN, NO CHIVALRY TO THE WEAKER SEX."

Shah Jahan himself made a triumphal entry into Orchha, the capital of the Bundelas, demolished the lofty and massive temple of Bir Singh Dev and raised a mosque in its place. Two sons and one grandson of Jujhar Singh who were of tender age, were made Moslems. Another son of Jujhar Singh, Udaybhan and a minister, Shyam Dawa, had fled to Golconda where they were captured by Kutubul-Mulk and sent to Shah Jahan. Udaybhan and Shyam Dawa were offered the alternative of Islam or death. Both chose the latter and were sent to the hell described in the Koran.

Shah Jahan was a notorious bigot.   His early hatred of Christians had been noticed by Sir Thomas Roe.   After his accession he grew averse to giving high posts to Rajputs who were Hindus.   The demolition of Hindu temples and desecration of images mark his reign only to a less extent than his son

TAJ MAHAL, A SHIVA TEMPLE

Aurangzib's.   He refused to release the Hindu Rajah of Dhamdhera (Malwa) from prison for a ransom of Rs 50,000 and insisted on his turning Moslem as the price of his liberation.

SHAH JAHAN ALSO COMMANDEERED THE FAMOUS SHIVA TEMPLE OF AGRA KNOWN AS TEJO MAHALAYA BELONG-ING TO THE MAHARAJA OF JAIPUR. HE COVERED THE EDIFICE WITH OUTER STONE COATING-WALLS WITH KORANIC INSCRIPTIONS AND TURNED THE TEMPLE OF LORD AGRESHWAR INTO A SO CALLED MAUSOLEUM AND NAMED IT THE TAJ MAHAL. Pandit P.N. Oak's research work on this subject is irrefutable. Several beautiful palaces belonging to the Hindus were similarly commandeered by the Moslem rulers and turned into Imambaras as can be seen in Lucknow, even today. Thus some of the Hindu edifices were saved from complete destruction (unlike the Krishna Temple of Mathura, the Vishwanath Temple in Benares or the great temples of Dwaraka and Somnath and Puri), but were instead covered up like the Imambaras and the Taj Mahal. Please see Index II for more information on the subject. The picture of Taj Mahal or Tejo-Mahalaya shown has been published on the 1983 calendar of the Amar Jyoti Ashram, Boulder, Colorado with the legend mentioned on the picture.

Shah Jahan was imprisoned by his son Aurangzib in the fort of Agra before his death. The old man at first held out and did not give in to his son who cut off the supply of water from the Jumna river. The old man was dying of thirst and eventually capitulated. At that time, he wrote to his fanatically Islamic son:

> Praised be the Hindus in all cases,
> As they ever offer water to their dead.
> And thou, my son, art a marvelous Musalman,
> As thou causest me in life to lament for (lack of) water!

q) AURANGZIB

Aurangzib became the king after Shah Jahan. In the process he murdered two of his brothers held in captivity and banished the third to the Arakan Hills to die in the hands of hillmen there. Aurangzib was an infidel-baiter of exceptional hatred. HE USED TO DESTROY ALL NON-MOSLEM HOUSES OF WORSHIP IN INDIA AND SEND MONEY TO THE SHERIF OF MECCA, THE HOLY CITY OF ISLAM. Those were the days when there was no oil wealth in the desert kingdom and the faithful had to eke out a precarious living from the pilgrims' contributions. Aurangzib's heart went out to help the Moslem mullahs of that distant holy land. However, he soon stopped his direct contribution after a few payments when he became suspicious about the actual disbursements going elsewhere and not to the needy. He made some attempts to help the needy of Arabia directly himself through an agency and not through the Sherif of Mecca any more.

Aurangzib had started his life of an infidel-baiter long before he ascended the throne. In 1645 A.D. he destroyed the temple of Chintaman in Gujarat and built a mosque on top of it, with the same building material obtained from the demolished temple. On hearing that the Hindus had rebuilt some of the temples destroyed by him earlier, he sent his order as the king to the Moslem governor of Gujarat: "In Ahmedabad and other areas of Gujarat in the days before my accession, temples were destroyed by my order. They have been repaired and idol-worship resumed. Carry out the former order."

In 1666 A.D. he ordered the police chief of Mathura, a holy Hindu city, to remove a stone railing which had been presented by Dara Shikoh, his elder brother and son of Shah Jahan, to the temples of Keshav Rai. HE EXPLAINED: "IN THE MOSLEM FAITH IT IS A SIN EVEN TO LOOK AT A TEMPLE AND THIS DARA HAD RESTORED A RAILING IN A TEMPLE!"

A general policy toward Hindu temples was proclaimed in April, 1669. Maasir-i-Alamgiri records: "It has reached the ears of His Majesty, the protector of the faith, that in the provinces of Thatta, Multan and Benares, especially in the latter, foolish Brahmans were in the habit of expounding frivolous books in their schools and that students, Moslems as well as Hindus, went there, even from great distances, led by a desire to become acquainted with the wicked sciences they taught. The Director of the Faith, consequently, issued orders to all governors of provinces to destroy with a willing hand the schools and temples of the kafirs and they were strictly enjoined to put an entire stop to the teachings and practices of idolatrous forms of worship. IT WAS REPORTED THAT IN OBEDIENCE TO HIS ORDER, THE GOVERNMENT OFFICERS HAD DESTROYED THE FAMOUS TEMPLE OF VISHWANATH AT BENARES."

Maasir-i-Alamgiri continues: "In the month of Ramazan (January, 1670 A.D.) this justice-loving monarch, the constant enemy of tyrants, commanded the destruction of the Hindu temple of Mathura known by the name of Dehra Keshav Rai, and soon the stronghold of falsehood was levelled to the ground. On the same spot was laid, with great expense, the foundation of a vast mosque . . .GLORY BE TO ALLAH WHO HAS GIVEN US FAITH OF ISLAM THAT IN THIS REIGN OF THE DESTROYER OF FALSE GODS, AN UNDERTAKING SO DIFFICULT OF ATTAINMENT HAS BEEN BROUGHT TO A SUCCESSFUL CULMINATION. THE RICHLY JEWELED IDOLS, TAKEN FROM THE INFIDELS' TEMPLES WERE TRANSFERRED TO AGRA AND THERE PLACED BENEATH THE STEPS LEADING TO THE NAWAB BEGUM SAHIB'S (JAHANARA'S) MOSQUE IN ORDER THAT THEY MAY BE PRESSED UNDER FOOT BY THE TRUE BELIEVERS. MATHURA'S NAME WAS CHANGED TO ISLAMABAD AND THIS WAS THE NAME THAT WAS USED IN ALL OFFICIAL DOCUMENTS."

In the same year Sitaramji temple at Soron was destroyed as also the shrine of Devi Patan at Gonda; news also came from Malwa that the local governor had sent 400 troopers to destroy all temples around Ujjain. The order was: "Every temple built during the last 10 or 12 years should be demolished without delay. Also, do not allow the despicable Hindu infidels to repair their old temples. Reports of the destruction of temples should be sent to the court under the seal of the Kazis (Moslem judges) and attested by pious Shaikhs."

BHAI MATI DASS BEING SAWED ALIVE

In Mathura, not being able to take this kind of persecution, the Jats rebelled. The Jat leader Gokla and his family were taken prisoner. The Jat leader's limbs were hacked off one by one on the platform of the police office of Agra, his family forcibly converted to Islam, and his followers were kept in prison in charge of the provost of the imperial camp.

In 1672 A.D. several thousand Satnamis were slaughtered near Narnaul in Mewat and in 1675 A.D. Sikh Guru Tegh Bahadur was tortured and finally beheaded for his resistance to forcible conversion of the Hindus in Kashmir. His disciples were slaughtered in front of him to frighten the Guru. The pictures on pages 42, 44 and 46 show the manners in which the disciples were murdered. The beheading of Guru Tegh Bahadur is shown on the front cover of the book.

The special tax called the 'jiziya' was reimposed on the Hindus and other non-Moslems after a lapse of several years. The Hindus of Delhi organized a peaceful protest and presented their case to the emperor while he was on his way to the mosque. AURANGZIB ORDERED HIS ELEPHANTS TO BE DRIVEN THROUGH THE MASS OF PEOPLE TRAMPLING MANY TO DEATH.

It was specially during the reign of Aurangzib that the moral degeneration of Moslem gentry became unbearable to the kafirs. The prime minister's grandson, Mirza Tafakhkhur used to sally forth from his mansion in Delhi with his ruffians, plunder the shops in the bazaar or market, kidnap Hindu women passing through public streets in litters or going to the river for bath and prayers, and dishonor them; and yet there was no judge to punish him or his friends, no police to prevent such crimes. Everytime such an occurrence was brought to the attention of the emperor, he referred the matter to the prime minister and nothing was done. At last after a Hindu artilleryman's wife had been forcibly abducted and his comrades threatened mutiny, Aurangzib merely ordered the licentious youth to be prevented from coming out of the mansion.

In Aurangzib's time in particular, the settled principle of Islam ended by making the Moslems a privileged class, nourished on state bounties taxed from the kafirs. The Moslems became

A SIKH DISCIPLE BEING BURNT ALIVE

indolent in peace time and unable to stand on their own legs in the arena of life. Public office came to be regarded as the birthright of the Moslems and so every inducement to display superior ability or exertion was taken away from them. The enormous areas of land given away by Moslem kings as grants to mosques and other Islamic institutions, nourished thousands of Moslem families in a life of slothful ease, while the natural increase of every succeeding generation turned their competence into deepening squalor. The vast sums spent by the Islamic state in maintaining Moslem poor houses and scattering alms during Ramazan and other Moslem holy days, were a direct premium on laziness. It was more lucrative to be a 'faqir' (beggar calling Allah in the street) at the capital than to earn an honest living as a cultivator, subject to the caprices of the seasons and the worst caprices of the revenue underlings and officials on tour. Thus a lazy and pampered class was created in the empire, who sapped its strength and was the first to suffer when its prosperity was arrested. Wealth bred indolence and love of ease; these soon led to vice; and vice finally brought about ruin to the followers of Allah. The kafirs of course had to bear the entire burden of these parasites all along.

Although Aurangzib hated idolatry, he used to go round the pretended foot-prints and hair of the prophet Mohammed, as if these were representations of the Deity. From his death-bed he wrote letters to his warring sons Azam and Kam Bakhsh advising them not to fight and to cultivate brotherly love which the emperor himself was unable to do in his life time. Aurangzib's another name was Alamgir (conqueror of the world) and many used to say about him: "Alamgir - zinda pir", meaning Alamgir is a living saint, referring to his highly religious and Islamic conduct, an attribute that failed to generate brotherly love in him. Blood, hatred, fire and sword, cunning and subterfuge were his instruments for spreading the message of his religion and the edifice naturally did not last long.

The kafirs had a terrible time under the Moslem king Aurangzib. A learned Kazi called Mughis-ud-din had declared that in accordance with the teachings of the Islamic jurisprudence: "The Hindus are designated in the Moslem law as 'payers of tribute' (kharaj-guzar); and when the revenue officer

BHAI DYALA BEING BOILED ALIVE

demands silver from them, they should without question and with all humility and respect, tender gold. If the officer throws dirt into their mouths, they must without reluctance open their mouths wide to receive it. By these acts of degradation are shown the extreme obedience of the 'zimmi', the glorification of the true faith of Islam, and the abasement of false faiths. Allah Himself orders them to be humiliated, as He says, 'till they pay 'jiziya' with the hand and are humbled."

Aurangzib had a queer sense of humor. He used to tell his temple-destroying soldiers that there was no need to hurry. They could take their time as the temples could not go away and escape by themselves. Aurangzib got his elder brother Dara Shikoh murdered by his harem eunuchs. Murad, another brother was invited to dinner, drugged with a somniferous potion and finally arrested and murdered. Dara's beheaded body was paraded in the streets of Delhi on the back of an elephant. Dara's children were also murdered by opium poisoning in the state prison at the orders of Aurangzib. His own son, Muhammad Sultan, who once rebelled against the father, was poisoned slowly with opium in the prison at Gwalior.

Even for Allah, such actions were hard to take. Only two centuries later a grim fate overtook the sons and grandson of the last Moslem emperor of Delhi when in 1857 they were shot in cold blood by an English soldier, while the royal heirs were vainly protesting their innocence and crying for an inquiry into their past conduct. The place they were executed is not too far from Humayun's tomb.

Aurangzib, on ascending the throne of Delhi, declared himself the 'Khalifa' or caliph of the entire Moslem world. He thus did not give his recognition to the caliph of Turkey who had been considered by many as the temporal leader of all Moslems. It is an inscrutable twist of fate that several centuries later, a Hindu named Mohandas Karamchand Gandhi, born and brought up among the Moslems of Gujarat, would declare his faith in the caliph of Turkey as the temporal leader of all Moslems, when most of the Islamic world had already renounced their allegiance to this potentate.

r)   ABDALI

This Afghan Moslem invader attacked India and destroyed the Hindu holy city Mathura once again after all the ravages done by his predecessors. His sacking of Mathura, the Bethlehem of the Hindus, is worth recounting. After having killed thousands of Hindus on his way, he finally arrived at the holy city. The invader had issued his orders to sally and plunder (March 3, 1757 A.D.). His soldiers were assured that everyone would be allowed to keep whatever plunder he took and would be paid Rs 5 (a sizeable amount at the time) for every enemy head brought in. It was midnight when the camp-followers went out to attack. One horseman mounted a horse and took ten to twenty others, each attached to the tail of the horse preceding it, and drove them just like a string of camels. When it was three hours after sunrise they were seen to come back. Every horseman had loaded up all his horses with the plundered property, and atop of it rode the girl-captives and the slaves. The severed heads were tied up in rugs like bundles of grain and placed on the heads of the captives. . .Then the heads were stuck upon lances and taken to the gate of the chief minister for payment. It was an extraordinary display! Daily did this manner of slaughter and plundering proceed. And at night the shrieks of the women captives who were being raped, deafened the ears of the people. . .All those heads that had been cut off were built into pillars, and the captive men upon whose heads those bloody bundles had been brought in, were made to grind corn, and then their heads too were cut off. These things went on all the way to the city of Agra, nor was any part of the country spared. . .Ahmed Shah Abdali also destroyed the holiest temple of the Sikhs in Amritsar. To desecrate the holy Golden temple, he slaughtered hundreds of cows and filled the sacred tank of the temple with the cows' blood.

s)   TIPU SULTAN

Tipu was another Moslem ruler who claimed to be a good believer and so quoting from the Koran used to carry out abhorrent practices such as whipping in public, cutting away limbs of kafirs and burying them alive, stoning to death and beheading on the slightest pretext.

Tipu's well-known boast was: "I am the chosen servant of prophet Mohammed, predestined in the eternal book of fate to root out the infidels from India and cast them into the bottomless pit of hell." He used to capture the children of the Europeans and when he felt the urge, he ordered them out of the dungeons into his private chamber. There, he defecated and urinated upon them, lashed them, hung them over slow-burning fires, and having drugged them to insensibility, murdered each by decapitation. Sometimes he would employ a pair of Abyssinian slaves who would twist the children by the heads and legs to death.

Tipu forcibly circumcised thousands of Hindus and compelled them to eat cow-meat, a monstrous act of impiety. He once seized two thousand Nair women and delivered them to his troops as prostitutes. His rule became unbearable to the non-Moslem population living in his kingdom.

t)   SIRAJ-UD-DAULA

At the age of twenty years Siraj-ud-daula had already made the life of his Hindu subjects quite miserable. It was at the hands of the British that this 'lion of Islam' met with defeat and made an attempt to escape in disguise. He was captured and brought to Murshidabad, where the British, unlike the Hindus, cut him to pieces and paraded his remains through the streets on an elephant before throwing them to the dogs in the street. Thus ended the uneventful Islamic rule of fifteen months headed by this young king.

u)   YAHYA AND ZULFIKHAR ALI BHUTTO

Only recently the Islamic government of Pakistan enacted similar dramas in Bangladesh, erstwhile East Pakistan. It was 1971 A.D. and while negotiations were still in progress between the two wings of Pakistan, the Moslem government of West Pakistan UNLEASHED A SURPRISE ATTACK ON THE UNARMED POPULATION OF EAST PAKISTAN.

Throughout the long night three battalions of soldiers (one infantry, one artillery and one armored) killed defenseless Dacca Bengalis with bayonets, rifles, machine guns, mortars, artillery pieces, rockets, flame throwers and tanks. The targets were: Dacca University, the police barracks, Sheikh Mujib's home, the radio station, offices of pro-Mujib newspaper and of course HINDU HOMES. Several hundred young men, the cream of the country were mowed down at the Dacca University. AT THE HINDU STUDENTS' DORMITORY, THE STUDENTS WHO SURVIVED THE ATTACK WERE FORCED TO DIG GRAVES FOR THEIR SLAUGHTERED FELLOW STUDENTS, EXACTLY LIKE THE 800 JEWS OF QURAYZA, AT THE TIME OF MOHAMMED, THE PROPHET OF ISLAM. Then they too were shot and stuffed into the graves dug with their own hands. THOUSANDS OF HINDUS DIED THAT NIGHT. MORE THAN THREE HUNDRED MOSLEM TROOPS ATTACKED THE GIRL STUDENTS OF ROCKEY HALL, DACCA UNIVERSITY. STRIPPING THEM NAKED, THE TROOPS RAPED, BAYONETED, AND MURDERED LOVELY BENGALI GIRLS. Dozens of girls jumped to their death from the roof of the building rather than suffer the fate of their sisters.

Simultaneously with the attack in Dacca, other units of the Islamic Pakistani army smashed into cities and towns across the country. They followed the same scenario now perfected over the years: kill, rape, loot and burn. THE SECOND ATTACK LAUNCHED AFTER A CALCULATED WAIT BY THE PAKISTANI ARMY IN ANOTHER COLD-BLOODED ORGY OF KILLING, RAPE, PLUNDER AND ARSON, SMASHED THE COUNTRY'S MAIN POPULATION CENTERS. WORKING FROM CAREFULLY PREPARED LISTS, SPECIAL COMMANDO UNITS OF THE ISLAMIC STATE HUNTED DOWN AND EXTERMINATED ALL BENGALI LEADERS, INTELLECTUALS, PROFESSORS, STUDENTS, DOCTORS, LAWYERS, JOURNALISTS AND HINDUS, THE PRIME TARGET OF ALL. THE TALES OF BUTCHERY AND BRUTALITY WERE ENDLESS.

As the killings continued on land, Pakistani jets strafed and rocketed defenseless villages. Strong mechanized units moved out to execute a different kind of raid or 'ghazzua' making them 'ghazis' too. The message of the Koran was interpreted in a devious way. One would say that Allah did not like this conduct from His followers and so eventually victory was snatched away from the hands of Islamic Pakistan. The kafirs of India not only defeated the Pakistanis but captured 90,000 of these ruffians passing off as soldiers. And, the soft-hearted kafirs did not even try these murderers and punish those among them who were guilty of such heinous crimes against humanity, but let them go scot free, without even making a few go to jail for a day. This act of misplaced kindness stands in great contrast with the treatment meted out to helpless, unarmed Hindu prisoners, hundreds and thousands of them, who were summarily butchered by the Moslem kings, in the name of Islam. The few Hindu and Sikh prisoners that Pakistan had captured were of course liquidated right away for Pakistan failed to return them saying that they had no Hindu prisoners in their hands, worth the mention.

That Allah did not listen to the prayers of the believers after this dastardly incident is also proven by the fact that the main actor in the drama, Zulfikhar Ali Bhutto, was himself hanged later by his own countrymen. And the then president of Pakistan, a general named Yahya, was dismissed and died a death devoid of glory or satisfaction because the land of Islamic Pakistan became very much reduced as a result of the diabolical enterprise of imperialism, slaughter, loot, arson and murder undertaken by Pakistan.

v) SOMETHING TO THINK ABOUT

Moslems in India and elsewhere have been led to believe by mullahs and Moslem 'historians' that the conquest of India by Islam started with the invasion of Sindh by Muhammad bin Qasim in 712 A.D.; it was resumed by Mahmud of Ghazni in 1000 A.D. and completed by Mohammed Ghori when he defeated the Chauhans of Ajmer-Delhi and Gahadvadas of Kanauj in the last decade of the 12 century.

Moslems of India have been persuaded to look back with pride on those six centures, if not more, when India was ruled by Islamic kings. In this make-belief, the British rulers are treated as temporary intruders who cheated Islam of its Indian empire for a hundred years, and the kafir Hindu, who succeeded the British in 1947 A.D., as usurpers of what rightfully belongs to Islam.

If we compare the Arab struggle on the frontiers of India with their record elsewhere we will see some difference. Within eight years of their prophet's death, they had conquered Persia, Syria and Egypt. By 650 A.D. they had advanced up to the Oxus river and the Hindu-Kush range. Between 640 and 709 A.D. they had reduced the whole of North Africa. They had conquered Spain in 711 A.D. But it took them 70 long years to secure the first foothold on the soil of India. No historian worth his name should have the cheek to say that the Hindus have always been an easy game for the invaders. THE HINDUS' HUMANITARIANISM PLAYED A GREAT PART IN GIVING UNNECESSARY ENCOURAGEMENT TO THE MOSLEMS AND THE INDO-PAKISTAN WARS, ALL THREE OF THEM PROVED THAT THE KAFIR CAN HOLD HIS OWN AGAINST ANY ISLAMIC INVADER.

SPAIN, GREECE AND ITALY HAVE ALL THROWN THEIR MOSLEM INVADING POPULATIONS OUT AND THERE IS NO REASON TO BELIEVE THAT THE SAME WILL NOT HAPPEN ON THE INDIAN SUBCONTINENT IF THE SITUATION SO DEMANDS. Times have changed but the lessons of history should not be forgotten. The past is not only history; it is also a prophecy.

Footnotes

1.   Compare this with the liberation of 90,000 Pakistani soldiers that committed incredible crimes in East Pakistan.

2.   The word Hindu-kush stems also from the fact that many Hindus were butchered by the Moslems on that Himalayan range at the time.

CHAPTER 10

ISLAM IN ACTION II

Islam appeared on the world scene some 600 years after the birth of Christianity. By the time Mohammed proclaimed himself a prophet in 610 A.D., Christianity had already spread over those countries in Europe, Asia and Africa which had formed parts of the Roman Empire at the height of its expansion. One would say that the desert of Arabia did not count for much in the eyes of the Christian missionaries. Some however had visited the southern parts of the peninsula and made some converts. But the 'chosen ones' had been left to live alone in the company of Arab 'heathen' and the 'accursed Jew' who had quite a few colonies in the oases spread over the central and northern parts of the desert. Little did the Christian missionaries suspect that the 'heathens' of Arabia were to challenge very soon the dictates of the Christian Church.

'Islam' is derived from the Arabic word 'salam' and has been presented to mean 'peace' or 'surrender', depending upon the time and place of presentation. IN A COUNTRY AND AT A TIME WHERE AND WHEN MOSLEMS ARE NOT IN POWER, IT IS PRESENTED AS 'PEACE'. BUT AS SOON AS THE MOSLEMS BECOME DOMINANT IT MEANS 'SURRENDER', AND THAT TOO AT THE POINT OF THE SWORD. The surrender is supposed to be made to Allah the only God according to Islam. But Allah is sure to spurn the surrender unless it is preceded by a surrender to the prophet, the sole spokesman for Allah. In effect, it means a surrender to whichever mullah happens to be hailed as authentic interpreter of the Koran and the Hadis, in the eyes of the sultan who wields the sword, the sole arbiter in matters moral and spiritual. In fact, even in Islamic jurisprudence, the Arabic word 'faisalah' which means 'settlement' is derived from the word 'faisal' which means 'sword'. While Jesus was not the founder of the Christian Church and had nothing to do with the dogmas of Christianity, the 'umm' or 'millat', which means 'society', became the vehicle of Islam. The 'millat' was founded and given a finished form, as well as a fanatic ideology, by Mohammed himself. Again, while the personality, preachings and performance of Jesus can be pitted against the Church and its dogma, there is little in Islam which is not derived directly from the personality, preachings and performance of its prophet.

a)   ALLAH AND HIS PROPHET

What exactly happened to Mohammed in the mountain cave outside Mecca has remained a controversial question. We are told by the theologians of Islam that his 'experience' is not verifiable by any other human being, nor his 'revelation' subject to human reason. One has to accept Mohammed's word that he was the 'last' and the 'most perfect' prophet, and that whatever he said or did in a state of 'wahi' (trance) or otherwise was the pronouncement and precription from 'almighty' Allah.

Those who took Mohammed at his word and accepted his prophethood were acclaimed by him as 'momins' while those who rejected his mission were denounced as kafirs. The word 'momin' means 'believer' in Mohammed and Allah. The 'momins' did not have to be better men than the kafirs in terms of consciousness or character. They had only to recite the 'kalima' (incantation) - 'there is no god but Allah, and Mohammed is His prophet' - and they become qualified to kill as many kafirs as they could or pleased, looting and burning their belongings and enslaving their women and children in the process.

Allah himself had been a part of the Arab pantheon at Mecca for many centuries past. He had shared his divinity with a large number of other gods and goddesses worshipped by the Arabs in Mecca, though he enjoyed a certain primacy. The bedouin, who roamed the desert, flocked to Mecca at appointed times for pilgrimage, and worshipped his gods and goddesses with whatever offerings he could spare from his meager possessions. Neither the bedouins nor the settled citizens of

Arabia had ever suspected that their Allah was soon going to become the sole cock of the walk and the cause of a bloody and prolonged strife in many parts of the world.

It is also debatable why Mohammed chose Allah alone, out of a large-sized Arab pantheon. He could have easily bestowed this singular honor on any other god or goddess in Mecca, or in the temple of some other town in Arabia. The gods and goddesses had obviously no choice in the matter. THE ONLY RATIONAL EXPLANATION IS THAT THE SOUND OF THE NAME ALLAH WAS NEAR TO THE SOUND OF ELOHIM[1] , THE GOD OF THE JEWS. Jesus had also cried out to Eli before he died on the cross. There are too many Judaic elements in Islam to rule out this explanation. But whatever the reason for Mohammed's choice, there is no reason to doubt that Allah would not have assumed the status he did without the help of Mohammed. It is small wonder that Allah in his turn felt so tender toward Mohammed, and proclaimed the latter to be the last and the most perfect prophet in human history.

Things started happening soon after the covenant between Allah and his only prophet was struck in the mountain cave outside Mecca, through the good offices of an angel named Gabriel. The 'Qurayza' who were the dominant tribe in Mecca would not have minded a number of their clan acclaiming Allah as the only God. They were used to such prophets appearing in Mecca and other Arabian towns, every now and then. They were a liberal people in matters of religion and did not mind how a man fancied himself or his God. But they were painfully surprised by the proclivities of this new prophet. He had started frequenting the forum outside the kaaba to denounce, in a rather strong language, all that they had cherished so far - their gods and goddesses, their cultural traditions, their social system, and what not - day in and day out.

Moslem mullahs have made a martyr out of Mohammed during his 12 years of prophethood at Mecca. They have explained away or justified the vindictiveness of Mohammed toward his own people of 'Qurayza' by citing the 'many injustices including violence' which Mohammed had 'suffered' at Mecca. No contemporary records of the 'Qurayza' have survived to tell the other side of the story. But there is enough evidence in the contemporary Islamic record to clinch the issue as to who was the aggressor and who the aggressed against. Here was a man sending all ancestors of the Arabs, including his own mother and father, to an eternal hell, and promising the same hell to the present and future generations of the Arabs, unless they accepted him as the only prophet of the only Allah. The 'Qurayza' would have been a dead people indeed if they had not reacted, and told Mohammed to leave their city for wherever he could find a more attentive audience.

It is for this 'crime' of the 'Qurayza' that Moslem mullahs have blackened the religion and culture of pre-Islamic Arabia as 'jahiliya' or ignorance. THE MULLAHS FORGET THAT THE ARABIC LANGUAGE WHICH IS THEIR PROUD POSSES-SION IN THE KORAN AND THE HADIS WAS NOT INVENTED BY THEIR PROPHET AT THE MOMENT, NOR 'REVEALED' BY ALLAH OUT OF THE BLUE. The rich language had a long ancestry, and reflected the genius of a culture which was deep as well as endowed with diverse dimensions. The pre-Islamic Arabs were a pagan people who allowed a god or goddess each according to his or her need and who respected worship from each according to his or her capacity. They had many other qualities of head and heart which the post-Islamic Arab society and culture came to lose progressively. A glimpse of pre-Islamic Arabia is given in appendix IV.

Islam professes to have brought peace to the warring tribes of Arabia. But its own chronicles tell of nothing except wars, more fierce than ever before, which the Arabs fought, first among themselves, and later on with their near and distant neighbors on all sides, soon after they were forced to surrender to Islam.

b)   THE 'MOMINS' AND THE KAFIRS

If we leave aside the myths and legends which Islam borrowed from Judaism - lock, stock and barrel - the message of Islam was very simple, almost simplistic.

To start with, it divided the Arabian society in two tight compartments, the 'momins' and the kafirs. The 'momins' were asked to muster together into a militant 'millat' - armed to the teeth, and ready to use force and/or fraud according as occasion demanded. The 'millat' surprised the settlements and the caravans of the kafirs in a series of armed raids or 'ghazzuas'. The kafirs who were always caught unawares had no choice but to surrender, many a time without a single skirmish. The swordsmen of the 'millat' selected and slaughtered, in cold blood, all kafirs who were capable of bearing arms. The movable and immovable property of the kafirs were appropriated by the 'millat'. The women and children of the kafirs were captured and sold as slaves or freed for ransom, after members of the 'millat' had their pick of the maidens.

Once in a while, the 'millat' discovered that the kafirs were in no mood to surrender in spite of the surprise, and that the armed conflict might turn out to its disadvantage. Then the 'millat' made overtures of peace on the condition that the kafirs got converted to Islam. The lives and families of the converts were spared but not their properties which were taken away as booty.

The mullahs take pride that Islam did away with tribal ties and united all Arabs in one brotherhood. It must be admitted that the 'millat's' method of doing away with tribal ties was very effective indeed. Quite often one or several members of a family or tribe happened to be 'momins', while their other kinsmen were ranged against them as kafirs. The 'millat' encouraged a brother to engage his brother in armed combat, so that one of them was sure to get killed. In case of kafirs who had to be slaughtered after the war, the 'millat' searched its own ranks for the nearest kinsmen to perform the 'pious' deed. A 'momin' was supposed to retain or recognise no relationship except that of a common creed. All other humanities were now rendered irrelevant.

The 'momins' were not of course risking their lives for nothing. Four-fifths of the booty and prisoners captured in war was theirs in accordance with a 'law' laid down by the prophet himself. The prisoners included quite a number of fair and young maidens who could set any 'momin's' mouth watering. No wonder that the infant state of Islam at Medina was able to assemble very soon quite a number of 'dedicated' swordsmen without spending a penny from its own coffers. The principle

of free enterprise applied to plunder and pillage was function-
ing with full force.

In case a 'momin' got killed in the 'holy war', he was promised
a permanent place in heaven. The Koran said: "They shall
recline on jeweled couches face to face, and there shall wait
on them immortal youths with bowls and ewers and a cup of
purest wine (that will neither pain their heads nor take away
their reason); with fruits of their own choice and flesh of fowls
that they relish. And theirs shall be dark-eyed houris, chaste
as hidden pearls: a guerdon for their deeds." According to one
tradition, quoted by Will Durant, each 'momin' was promised 72
of these houris, who would never age or stop being solicitous.
According to other traditions, the number could be many times
more. It was surely an added attraction.

The balance one-fifth of the booty and prisoners of war were
assigned to the Islamic state which the prophet had set up at
Medina to start with, and which moved to other cities in due
course, under the caliph or 'amir-ul-mominin'. This one-fifth
had to be the pick of the bunch before members of a military
expedition could claim their share. No wonder that the
Islamic state at Medina was very soon rolling in riches. The
wealth which flowed to the Islamic state in later times grew
progressively in volume and variety, and the stage was set for
the flowering of that Islamic 'culture' in which the 'millat'
takes such mighty pride. The prophet and the earlier caliphs,
who controlled and commanded these riches, were inclined to
lead a life of 'poverty'. This 'piety' impressed the 'momins'
who had to be satisfied with much less, and served to create
many myths about Islamic 'ideal of equality'. The 'equality'
never made any difference to the despotic power which the
prophet and later on, the caliphs had at their disposal.

c)   SWEEP OF THE ISLAMIC SWORD

The prophet of Islam had proclaimed that Allah had assigned
the whole world to the 'millat'. Not a patch was to be left for
the kafirs to dwell. And no corner of the world was to be
bereft of mosques from which the 'muezzin' could call the
'faithful' to prayer. But it seems that Allah's knowledge of
geography was not so good. His prophet had not heard of many

lands beyond Syria, Iraq, Persia, Ethiopia and Egypt. He knew nothing of El Cid's Spain, or Conrad de Montferrat's France or the land of Richard the Lion-Hearted. He knew nothing about India and the Hindus which want of knowledge was to lead to an interesting theological controversy later on.

Notwithstanding this lack of geographical knowledge, the prophet divided the world into two contending spheres: 'darul-Islam' (the zone of peace where the Moslems were the dominant element) and 'darul-Harb' (the zone of war, where the non-Moslems or kafirs held sway). The inhabitants of 'darul-Islam', that is, the Moslems were commanded to wage unceasing war upon 'darul-Harb' till the latter was converted to 'darul-Islam'. The frontiers of the Islamic empire were to be pushed progressively in all directions. The theory of Islamic imperialism was thus perfected by the prophet himself, like the later-day theory of communist imperialism which Lenin elaborated as 'international proletarian revolution'.

The whole of Arabia had been terrorised into surrendering to the sword of Islam by the time the prophet passed away in 632 A.D. The militarised 'millat' which had 'elected' an 'amir-ul-mominin' in the same year, now started seeking fresh fields for the misson of Islam. Persia had exhausted herself in unceasing war with the Roman Empire. The provinces of the Roman Empire in Asia and North Africa were seething with rebellion against persecution of 'heresies' by the Church at Rome which had by now reduced every other ecclesiastical dispensation to a subordinate status. Persia and the Roman provinces fell in quick succession after the armies of Islam had first found out the feebleness of their defenses, and then delivered decisive blows.

Thus within a hundred years after the death of the prophet, the 'amir-ul-mominin' at Damascus became the master of a mighty empire, spread over Spain, Sicily, North Africa, Egypt, Palestine, Syria, Iraq, Persia, Khorasan and Sindh. It was a military triumph unprecedented in the annals of human history so far. The triumph could be easily explained in terms of political and military causes and consequences. But the mullahs chose to attribute it to the might of Allah which had been 'fully and finally thrown on the side of Islam'. Henceforth, there was no justification for anyone to dwell in the 'darkness of 'kufr''. The 'light' of Islam was now accessible to all.

The newly conquered countries were inhabited not by thinly spread out tribal settlements but by populous societies, urban and rural. It was no more possible for the 'momins' to kill all kafirs who rejected Islam or capture and carry away all their women and children. Besides, the properties the kafirs possessed, and the lands on which they lived were so voluminous and vast. The mullahs, therefore, developed a more elaborate theory of an Islamic state, out of the embryo of principles which the prophet had already propounded.

The 'millat' led by the 'amir-ul-mominin' was, of course, the master class under the Islamic state. But this state had a mission larger than providing power and privilege to the 'millat'. The state had to see to it that the kafirs who had been conquered were brought into the fold of Islam as fast as possible. The kafirs were, therefore, given a new status - that of 'zimmis' to start with. The 'zimmis' were allowed to live under the aegis of an Islamic state, provided they agreed to pay 'jiziya' (poll-tax) and other discriminatory taxes, and accepted a status of second class citizens placed under draconian disabilities. It was expected that the burden of taxes and the disgrace of disabilities would force the kafirs to get converted into Islam before long.

The expectation was more than fulfilled in most countries except Spain, Sicily and India. THE KAFIRS IN OTHER COUNTRIES WERE NOT ONLY CONVERTED TO ISLAM BUT WERE ALSO BRAINWASHED TO FULMINATE AGAINST THEIR ANCIENT HERITAGE, AND FORGET THAT THEY HAD BEEN CONQUERED BY A FOREIGN RACE AND CREED.

The mullahs applaud the concept of a 'zimmi' and describe it as a privileged position because, 'unlike the 'momins', the 'zimmis' are exempted from military service'. It is difficult to know how the mullahs arrived at this self-congratulatory conclusion. They certainly did not consult any kafir to find out if he wanted to become a 'zimmi' and be 'exempted' from military service. THE WHOLE THING WAS A DELIBERATE DEVICE ADOPTED IN ORDER TO DISARM AND EMASCU-LATE A SUBJECT POPULATION. People who could not bear arms were in no position to defend themselves against Islamic barbarities which became more pronounced with the passing of every day, in direct proportion to the establishment of 'salam' or 'peace' under the Islamic state.

The Islamic state allowed some time to the kafirs to 'mend' their ways and receive the 'true revelation'. But it had no patience for the religious and cultural institutions of the kafirs. IT SYSTEMATICALLY DESTROYED AND DESE-CRATED THE TEMPLES AND SHRINES OF THE KAFIRS, KILLED THEIR PRIESTS, BURNT THEIR SCRIPTURES AS WELL AS SECULAR LITERATURE, CLOSED THEIR SCHOOLS AND MONASTERIES AND HEAPED INSULT AND INJURY ON EVERY PRECEPT AND PRACTICE THAT THEY HAD CHERISHED SO FAR. It completed the job of 'cleaning up' the scene thoroughly. The conquered lands were at the same time 'adorned' with mosques and 'mazars'[2] in which the mullahs mugged up the Koran and the Hadis, the sufis ser-monised on the sublimation they had 'attained'.

d)   ISLAM: AN ALIBI FOR IMPERIALISM

For several centuries after its advent, Islam was an alibi for Arab imperialism. And it was an imperialism of a type which the world had not known so far. THE ARABS NOT ONLY IMPOSED THEIR RUTHLESS RULE AND TOTALITARIAN CREED ON THE COUNTRIES THEY CONQUERED; THEY ALSO POPULATED THESE COUNTRIES WITH A PROLIFIC PROGENY WHCH THEY PROCREATED ON NATIVE WOMEN. Every Arab worth his race 'married' scores, sometimes hun-dreds of these helpless women after their menfolk had all been killed. Divorce of a wedded wife had been made very easy by the 'law' of Islam. A man could go on marrying and divorcing at the rate of several women during the span of a single day and night. What was more convenient, there was no restric-tion on the number of concubines a man could keep. The Arab conquerors used these male privileges in full measure. And in a matter of a hundred years, Iraq, Palestine, Syria, Egypt and North Africa which had been non-Arab countries for countless ages became Arabic-speaking countries. Arabic did not spread like English, French or other similar languages that spread through commercial and diplomatic excellence of the lending nation and filtered through the top strata of the receiving countries. Arabic was injected through all strata of the conquered population which did not have much choice in the matter. Thus we have a series of countries that are 'Arabic' in race, culture and language extending from Iraq to Morocco. CONVERSION WAS NOT CONFINED TO CREED ALONE, IT COVERED ONE'S ANCESTRY AS WELL.

The Arab power declined in due course. The mission of Islam was next taken over by the Turks whom the Arabs had converted earlier. It was the Turks who succeeded where the Arabs had failed - conquering Asia Minor, invading Central Asia, India and Eastern Europe. ASIA MINOR WAS WRESTED FROM CHRISTIANITY, CONVERTED EN MASSE, AND POPULATED BY A PROLIFIC TURKISH PROGENY. IT IS KNOWN AS TURKEY TODAY. Central Asia, which was already Turkish, became Islamic as well. It was only in Eastern Europe and India that the Turks failed in the final round. But in both places, they crystallised colonies of native Moslems to carry forward the politics of conversion under changed circumstances. How far that politics will progress in the future depends upon whether the kafir societies in these lands understand it or not, at present.

Footnotes

1. See appendix IV for another view.

2. 'Mazar': Tomb

CHAPTER 11

ISLAM IN ACTION III

a)   KAFIR-KUSHI A LA SURAH VIII, VERSE 12

Around 1689 A.D. the Hindu king Shambhaji, son of Shivaji, was captured by Aurangzib's men. The Hindu king was murdered along with his minister Kavi Kalash. There are many ways of killing a defeated foe. Freeing a defeated foe after the battle, like the Hindu kings used to do or the Indian government did when they freed without trial the criminal elements of the Moslem Pakistani prisoners captured in the then East Pakistan (now Bangladesh), was of course unthinkable in Islamic ethics and more so if the foe was a kafir, an enemy of Allah and the prophet Mohammed. Kafirs were killed in a more sophisticated way, the way prescribed by the Koran. Chopping a kafir's head off at a single stroke of the sword or crushing his head in a single blow was considered too mild. The idea was to make the pain last, as long as possible. Thus in Islam's hell, a kafir burns but his skin goes on growing to be burnt continuously so that the pain becomes everlasting. Death is the termination of all pains and so it must be delayed to teach a lesson and to prove without fail the greatness of Allah's religion.

SHAMBHAJI WAS FIRST BLINDED AND KAVI KALASH'S TONGUE WAS PULLED OUT. ON MARCH 11, 1689, THEY WERE PUT TO A CRUEL AND PAINFUL DEATH. THEIR LIMBS WERE HACKED OFF ONE BY ONE AND THEIR FLESH THROWN TO THE DOGS.

It was in the year 1669 A.D. that the Hindu king Gokla was captured by Aurangzib. THE HINDU KING'S LIMBS WERE HACKED OFF ONE BY ONE ON THE PLATFORM OF THE POLICE STATION OF AGRA, THE CITY OF TAJ MAHAL.

63

HIS WHOLE FAMILY WAS FORCIBLY CONVERTED TO ISLAM.

One might think that such gruesome murders committed in accordance with the injunctions of the Koran are a thing of the past. But it is not so. The following incident proves it.

Bengal in pre-partition India was then being ruled by Suhrawardy, the Muslim League leader. Suhrawardy had laid a diabolical plan to destroy the Hindu city of Calcutta. One Mr. Haren Ghosh, a music teacher who used to give lessons in music to the girls of Suhrawardy's family, came to know of the plot and he informed the authorities. Calcutta was saved at the nick of time and eventually Suhrawardy came to know that his plans were divulged by his music teacher. Mr. Ghosh was kidnapped, his limbs were hacked off one by one and his cut up body was found in a box that was left in a Calcutta street. And this happened in the 1940's. Islam has not changed and those who think otherwise only fool themselves.

Even today the Sheikhs of Arabia make sick jokes when they ask their non-Moslem friends if they had a choice which one would they choose for their death: death by a single stroke severing the head or death by chopping their limbs off one by one.

b) ISLAM AND KAFIR WOMEN

The chapter on the Koran and Moslem women gives us some idea on Islam's injunctions on Moslem women. They should cover their bodies from head to foot. Khomeini's Iran forces the women to go under the 'chador'. They must not go outside to work where other men might see them. They may not be rulers or judges in an Islamic state. Women lawyers are frowned upon in today's Pakistan which is an Islamic state.

But such regulations are valid for Moslem women only. The non-Moslem or kafir women are to be handled differently, as the Islamic codes are not binding on them. The kafir women are considered to be the property of Moslems; they are their 'slaves' and the wife or daughter of a 'zimmi' can be molested by a Moslem with impunity in a Moslem state ruled by the

'Sharia' or Islamic jurisprudence. The idea comes from the treatment meted out to kafir women who were captured in the battlefield. The first fifth of all booty went to the prophet or the caliph or whoever happened to hold the position of the amir-ul-mominin. It could be the Moslem king of the land or even a petty chieftain. This so called leader 'examined' all booty, inspected and sometimes 'felt' by touching it. The women, all of them were paraded in front of the leader, naked or scantily clad, so that the leader could make his choice. These women were NOT brought in front of the 'amir-ul-mominin' dressed in 'chadors'. It was thus that the prophet himself used to inspect his captives and chose Rehana and Juwairiya, both Jewish women whose male relatives were all killed by the Moslems. Juwairiya eventually gave up her religion and married the prophet and became one of the ten or eleven wives of his harem. Rehana was a courageous lady and she did not give up her Jewish faith and so was turned into a concubine of the prophet. She thus took her place on the side of Mary, another slave woman, and a Christian, who after Khadija gave birth to a male child fathered by the prophet.

Although the number of legal wives for Moslems is limited to four, there is no limit to the number of concubines a faithful servant of Allah could have. The practice eventually gave rise to immense seraglios or 'harems' in Islamic lands. IN INDIA, THE CAPTIVE WOMEN OF THE KAFIRS WERE INSPECTED BY THE MOSLEM KINGS IN WOMEN'S MARKETS CALLED MINA BAZAARS (MARKETS OF PEARLS) WHERE NO MALES OTHER THAN THE KING AND HIS PALS WERE ALLOWED ENTRY. They used to choose their favorite girls for the night and then let them circulate among their Moslem friends.

These unfortunate women had usually a very sad end. Anyone who has visited the Mughal palaces and forts in India must have seen the steep tunnels from the 'harem' opening on to the waterway below. The women, once they were no longer required, were dropped through these tunnels the head first. Near the bottom of the tunnel, just above the waterline, is a big boulder which is supposed to be struck by the head when the body gets to the bottom. The kafir woman died then and there and later the body floated out at high tide.

In 1947 A.D. at the time of partition of India, the Moslems on the Pakistani side killed the Hindus and Sikhs of West Punjab. They then forced the Hindu and Sikh women to come out in the streets completely naked and took out a procession. No chadors or veils for kafir women. When the terrible news arrived in East Punjab, the Moslems of India had to undergo the same treatment and this put a stop to such dastardly behavior by the followers of Allah.

In Bangladesh, during the genocide of kafirs there perpetrated by the soldiers of Islamic Pakistan, Hindu women were taken captives and kept in the army barracks without clothes for the enjoyment of the 'believers'. Kafir women are to be treated as slaves of Moslems and the treatment is clearly indicated in the Koran and the Hadis.

Kidnapping of Hindu women by Moslem gangs was once a common feature in India. This led to many riots and many lives were lost. In Bangladesh today, it is practically impossible for Hindu girls to go out alone in the streets to attend to daily chores without being teased, insulted or kidnapped by the Moslem ruffians. The recent Hindi movie entitled Umrao Jan depicts the life of a singer named Umrao Jan. She sings very well and is a kind of high class prostitute. The movie features a number of songs and also shows how the inglorious life of Umrao Jan started. She was kidnapped by a bunch of Moslem ruffians who sold her to a Moslem woman brothel-keeper. Umrao Jan was shown to be a Moslem girl in the movie however. (But in real life most of the kidnappers were Moslem ruffians and the kidnapped were kafir women.)

A number of cases have happened where Moslems have dressed up as Hindus and then followed Hindu girls on their way to the river for the holy bath. On the way, they pounced upon these girls, kidnapped them, raped them and in some cases killed them. In many instances such incidents were unreported for fear of shame and loss of face.

c) THE WOMEN OF RAJASTHAN

Many battles were fought in Rajasthan in Northern India. The Moslem hordes attacked the Rajput kingdoms many times and the Rajputs fought back heriocally and defeated the Moslems over and over again. There never was any attack on the Moslem womenfolk or the non-combattants by the Rajputs. On the other hand, if the Rajputs lost in the battle, the Moslems let loose terror on the entire population. The Rajputs' houses of worship were destroyed, their women raped and carried away, their children taken away as bonded labor and all non-combattants murdered.

The Rajputs soon came to know the way of the Moslems. If it appeared that the battle could not be won, then they themselves killed their women and children, Masada style, and then went to fight with the Moslems until death. In many cases, the Rajput women took their own lives by taking poison and then jumping into a deep fiery pit. This was called the Jauhar Vrat or 'sacrifice of fire'. The men of course went out to fight and died to a man.

Now, the question is why did the women jump into the fire to be burnt alive when they were going to die of the poison anyway? The answer is simple. If the Moslems got hold of the dead bodies of the kafir women after victory in the battle, they would then rape even the dead bodies of these women. It was to prevent such 'desecration' of their own bodies after death by poison that the Rajput women used to jump into the pits of fire. Thus, when the Moslems finally came to the city, they did not find a single woman's body, dead or alive. A great disappointment!

Showing disrespect to a dead body is a typically Islamic trait. Displaying the cut off head, or cut up body to the public to generate terror in the minds of the public is an effective method of subduing an otherwise rebellious population. In Islamic states, one is forced to witness an execution often done in public. Lashing of men and women is also often displayed to the public and now-a-days in Pakistan they arrange a microphone near the mouth of the victim of such torture so that people at a distance could hear his cries.

Stoning to death of course has to be in public as otherwise all the furniture would get damaged.

d)   AFZAL KHAN'S CONCUBINES

Afzal Khan was a notorious womaniser and he had a 'haremful' of Hindu or kafir women. No one exactly knew how many women he had in his harem. It is estimated that he had some 300 Hindu women as slaves or concubines, not counting the legal Moslem wives that he wedded and divorced from time to time.

Afzal had to meet the great Hindu king Shivaji in a mortal encounter. Afzal eventually died in the hands of Shivaji and his forces were routed. It is said that Afzal Khan had a premonition about his death in the hands of Shivaji who was a great fighter. He decided to murder all his concubines before he set out to meet the Hindu king. He himself beheaded a great number of these unfortunate women.

When someone asked him, what if he returned safe and sound from his meeting with the Hindu king, this Moslem chief replied that he could procure for himself the same number of kafir women for his 'harem' on his return, perhaps even a great number and more beautiful ones in the bargain.

e)   BRICKING UP OF WOMEN AND CHIDREN

Anarkali

The Koran says in Surah IV, Verse 15 that guilty women should be confined to their house till death overtakes them. It is also called the punishment of 'char-diwari' or the 'four-walls'. In Islamic lands this is a well-known punishment.

The Mughal king Akbar once suspected a young dancer called Anarkali (pomegranate flower) of romance with his own son, Salim. He disapproved of this relationship as the old man wanted the girl for himself. He had to punish her as he would not even dare to punish his own son for this was his only son fathered after many tries and at the specific blessing of a holy man called Salim Chisti. But someone had to be punished and so it was the poor girl.

GURU'S SONS BEING BRICKED UP

The girl was bricked in and left there to die a slow death. Even today one can visit the place where Anarkali was murdered in this brutal manner. Her tomb is in Lahore, Pakistan.

The Daughters of the Hindu King Dahir

Dahir, the Hindu king of Sindh was defeated by the Moslems. The women of the royal family were all raped and carried away by the ruffians after a merciless carnage. However, the two young daughters were safely taken to West Asia for the Moslem king who had stayed back in his capital. The girls were presents from the general who had conquered Sindh.

The girls were supposed to be virgins which they were. But to spite the cruel, old sex-fiend, the girls said that they were no longer virgins and that they were made to have sex with the general before being sent to the king. The enraged king got his general murdered but later discovered that the girls had lied. They were punished by being placed inside a thick wall where they were left to die.

The Sons of Guru Gobind Singh

The Sikh Guru Gobind Singh who was eventually murdered by the Moslems had his two sons captured by the Mughals. These two boys were murdered the same way. Please see picture on page 69.

f)   THE TERROR TACTICS OF ISLAM

In order to terrorise the kafirs they were murdered in other ways too with a view to generating mortal fear in the minds of the infidels. Akbar, after a victory on the battlefield, used to get hold of the more prominent members of the kafir society and impale them publicly. Any visitor visiting the dead city of Sikandra once built by Akbar, will notice structures on either side of the road leading to Sikandra, on top of which lances were placed for impaling the kafirs. The great pain and the shrieks of the unfortunate victims scared the hell out of the Hindus who were forced to watch the gruesome scene, while the Moslems howled for joy.

Another method was to flay alive the victims. In fact, this practice is very much in vogue even today in the Moslem country of Afghanistan. In Islamic Turkey too this practice was widely followed. In Islamic Pakistan, the practice has given rise to the common threat: "I will skin you alive". Truly inscrutable are the ways of the faithful!

During the reign of Abdul Hamid II, called the 'great assassin', the Turks were responsible for the torture, robbery, slaughter and rape of thouands of Armenians. The marauding Bashi-Bazouks of this mad sultan were notorious for running down and ravishing women and girls while on horse-back. All Christian males that fell into their hands were forcibly cir-cumcised and sodomized.

The great festivity in El-Obeid upon the defeat of Hicks Pasha's infidel army is noteworthy. The mad Messiah, El-Mahdi, built a pyramid of the skulls of the Christian army. In a well near by, they threw the sex organs of the infidels. About ten thousand Christian soldiers were thus butchered.

During the Crusades too, the Christian soldiers who fell into the hands of the followers of Allah, had their penis cut off for every true believer had to destroy the generative power of the infidel before he could gain admittance into Allah's paradise. Castration of the infidel was not only an act of piety for the Moslems but one of shame to the kafir. The infidel's head was severed and placed between his thighs, the seat of dishonor.

During Mughal rule in India, captive Hindus were also tortured by infibulation or artificial phimosis (mobri, muzzling), elonga-tion of the prepuce or foreskin and constriction of the orifice, a painful punishment. With the Hindu women captives, often their vulva was sewed up. Other practices involved mutilation of the uterus by means of iron prongs, burning the breasts and excision of the clitoris. A VERY PAINFUL PUNISHMENT WAS SPLITTING THE PENIS OF A HINDU. THIS WAS CALLED SUB-INCISION.

g) MURDER OF SIKH GURUS AND THEIR DISCIPLES

Guru Arjun Dev, the Sikh Guru was murdered by the Mughal king Jahangir by forcibly making him sit on a red hot iron plate and then pouring hot sand over him.

The murder of Guru Tegh Bahadur was no less horrendous reminding one of the scenes of hell described in the holy Koran. Tegh ahadur was asked by the Moslem king to renounce his religion, the faith of Guru Nanak or Sikhism. He refused. Moslems tried to frighten him. They brought him to the prison in a cage like he was a wild animal. Three of his disciples were murdered in front of him. One was cut in two by sawing alive as shown in the picture on page 42. Another was boiled alive in a big cauldron (See page 46). And the third was wrapped up in a blanket and then set on fire (See page 44). The last fits the Koranic injunction prescribed in Surah XXII, Verses 19-22.

h) SODOMY AMONG THE BELIEVERS

The Koran tells us of boys graced with eternal youth who will attend the faithful in paradise. The practice of sodomy is frowned upon in the Koran if the act takes place between two Moslems. There is nothing mentioned about a Moslem sodomising an infidel. This seems to have the silent approval of Islam. Many European travelers and Christian missionaries, unfamiliar with sodomite propensities of many Moslems, suffered sexual molestation in Persia in the hands of even government officials.

During the Napoleonic war in Egypt, Marshal Jaubert wrote to General Bruix that: "Les Arabes et les Mameloukes ont traité quelques-uns de nos prisonniers comme Socrate traitait, dit-on, Alcibiade. Il fallait périr ou passer". (The Arabs and the Mamelukes have used some of our men captured by them like they say Socrates used Alcibiade. It was a case of letting them do it or die.)

Sheikh Nasr, the governor of Bushire, once said to an English missionary: "I stopped a caravan of Jews bound for Afghanistan, penetrating all forty of their females in one night. They protested that such action was an outrage, but I said the outrage was justified in that all of their offspring would be Moslems".

i)   INFILTRATION AND SUBTERFUGE

During the Crusades, the Christians had a rough time. Their humanitarianism made them an easy prey to the Moslem spies that had infiltrated into Christian ranks as Armenian Christians. No secret could thus be kept from the invading Saracen armies. The situation became so serious that the Christians had to take drastic action. The Christians had to employ the same cruel methods of the Moslems to get rid of the false Armenians.

One evening at dinner time, a bunch of Turkish prisoners were killed by slitting their throats. They were then spitted and the cooks set about roasting them. The camp was informed that some spies had been caught and they were being roasted on the skewer. The whole camp came running up to see if it was really true for the Moslems did not believe that the Christians, followers of the dictum of turning the other cheek, could really kill the spies that way. But behold! Nothing could be more true: the Turks were truly cooking over a hot fire. The next morning, all the spies had disappeared in horror, even without waiting for their wages.

j)   ATTACK ON THE US EMBASSY IN PAKISTAN

The diabolical nature of the attack on the US embassy became apparent after the fact. Some Moslems had attacked the holy shrine at Mecca and this enraged the Moslems of Pakistan against all non-Moslems. They just assumed that the attack was organised by the Americans. The following extract from Masurashram Patrika of India dated March 1982 will make one shudder in horror:

> "A typical Pakistani Islamic reaction reported in American papers was that while some Pakistanis themselves mounted an attack on the Kaaba, their compatriots back home, apparently angered by the assault, caught hold of some helpless American women and urinated in their

mouths, obviously believing that they were in fact dis-
charging an Islamic obligation against the kafirs and an
oblation to Allah".

CHAPTER 12

IMPERIALISM IN THE GARB OF ICONOCLASM

Islam's injunctions to its followers to destroy and insult the other religions are well-known. Churches and synagogues in Southern Europe and Middle Eastern countries that have been desecrated by the Moslems in the name of Islam are too many to cite. The story did not change in the case of the subcontinent of India either. Their houses of worship were destroyed, desecrated, the deities stolen and carried away to be ground to dust or placed below the steps leading to mosques to be trod upon by Moslem pilgrims. The idea has been to insult the kafirs.

Of late the followers of Islam seem to have a second thought on the pheonomenon. A new breed has appeared on the scene who can be called apologists or public relations men for Islam. In the early days, Islam did not need any apologists. Anything done in the name of Islam was already justified and there was no room for any guilt complex. When Aurangzib executed the sufi holy man Sarmad, he knew that no apologies were required. When he tortured the mullahs that had advised his son to rebel against the father, Aurangzib was certain that no apologies were needed.

But times have changed and people do think on their own, more so among non-Moslems. Among the Moslems, however, free thinking is taboo, where Islam is concerned. This explains why this religion did not have any reformers or thinkers to purify the creed as human civilization progressed. Whatever was supposed to have been said by the prophet more than a thousand years ago is supposed to hold good today in its entirety.

One such apologist of Islam writes in his 'The Life and Times of Sultan Mahmud of Ghazna': "The critics who accuse the Sultan of wanton bloodshed and reckless spoliation of Hindu temples forget that these so-called barbarities were committed in the course of legitimate warfare, when such acts were sanctioned by the practice of all the great conquerors of the world. Spoils captured from a defeated enemy have always been considered lawful property of the victorious army. In India, however, wealth was accumulated not only in the coffers of the kings, as in other countries, but also in the vaults of the temples, which were consecrated in the service of various deities. The consequence was that, while elsewhere the capture of the defeated monarch's treasury usually gratified the conqueror's lust for Mammon, in India temples were also ransacked to secure the piles of gold and precious stones in time. The religious considerations rarely carry weight with a conqueror, and the Sultan does not appear to have been influenced by them in his schemes of conquest".

Quite clearly the apologist calls a simple but ferocious raider a conqueror. A raider raids and goes away but a conqueror adds to the conquered country's new system of government, commerce and industry. William the Conqueror, Napoleon, Alexander the Great were conquerors who contributed considerable developments to the conquered countries. Not so with Islamic conquerors. They built mosques on top of the destroyed temples. They violated the women, took slaves, killed non-combattants. The breed of Islamic raiders cannot be called conquerors in the true sense of the word. They were grabbers and could not grow anything themselves. The spirit of robbery, greed, intolerance toward people of other faiths, characterize these raiders as a special breed of people and time has come to look upon them as such and take proper precautions before it is too late.

All non-Moslems have been extremely tolerant toward the Moslems. The offending mosques built on the foundations of destroyed temples, have been allowed to remain and the Hindus have built new temples near by for a Hindu is reluctant to destroy the house of worship of anyone. Unfortunately, such behavior is translated by many Moslems as proven superiority of their religion. They can destroy someone else's house of worship but others cannot do the same to theirs.

During the Pakistani attack on East Pakistan's Hindus, they destroyed many Hindu temples. It was not to rob the vaults of the temples but to spite the kafirs and prove the superiority of Islam. The inherent difference between Islam as a religion and any other religion is to be recognised. It is the behavior of the Moslem and his holy book that can provide the key to the Moslem psyche and his attitude to the non-Moslem world.

The attack on the kafir's religion has not been limited to physical demolition of the non-Moslem edifices only. The onslaught has been carried out at the spiritual level as well. The gods and goddesses of the kafirs have been vilified in grossest terms by the exponents of Islam. The editor of the Moslem Daily 'Morning News' of Calcutta once wrote a leading article on Lord Krishna, the Hindu God of preservation. Krishna was described as 'the Gay Lothario of Vrindaban' alluding to so called amorous associations between Krishna and the girls from many cow-herds' families. The not so informed Moslem editor did not bother to find out that the escapades he referred to could not be possible for Krishna was only twelve year old at the time. How precocious can a twelve year old be?

Take the case of Jesus Christ for instance. The greatness of Christ lies in his gentleness. His advice to turn the other cheek is the epitome of Christian behavior. But Khomeini of Iran has announced, on more than one occasion, in his speeches to the believers, that the Christians are erroneous in attributing these qualities to Jesus Christ. Christ, according to Khomeini, could never have advised to turn the other cheek for no true prophet is foolish enough to say such a thing. This was all concocted by the imperialist and Satanic infidels of Europe and America to subjugate the peoples of other lands.

The Moslems on the other hand cannot tolerate it if anyone doubts the words and deeds of their prophet, finds his moral behavior objectionable vis-à-vis women or his words irreconcilable to his deeds, etc. If anyone expresses doubt on Mohammed's climbing to Islam's paradise on the back of the winged horse called Barq, then it becomes a blasphemy.

The Moslem blames everyone for some kind of idolatry. The Hindus have their gods and goddesses from a big pantheon of deities. The Christians have their trinity and they call Jesus, the son of God. To a Moslem these are sacrilegeous attributes. But when it comes to adoring the hair of the prophet which is said to be stored in the Hazratbal mosque in Kashmir, then it is all right. No one can call it idolatry then! But for a Buddhist to show his veneration in front of the temple in Ceylon that houses the toe-nails of Buddha, is 'kufr'.

Naturally, it becomes very difficult to comprehend the psychology of the followers of Islam in these days of logic and reason.

CHAPTER 13

SLAUGHTER AND SLAVERY

Slavery is permitted in Islam. Slaves captured in war become the property of the victor. Just like any property, they could be sold or transferred. The owner has every right over the body and soul of his slave men and women. In Islamic countries slavery was practised as late as only a few years ago. It was a flourishing trade. Christian and Jewish women were prized items. African slaves were good for labor. Many were castrated (although castration of Moslems is banned in Islam) and employed as eunuchs in the harems. The slave market of Mecca, located very near the shrine of Kaaba, was closed down very recently due to the pressure of public opinion abroad.

Then there were the janissaries. These were the Christian youths captured by the Turks and forced to become Moslems and join the ranks of the Islamic army, after circumcision. Usually, as can be easily imagined, the slaves had a very rough time. Slavery went hand in hand with slaughter as one could have the slaves only by killing the husbands or fathers and brothers of the prospective slave men and women.

The Armenians had been massacred many times by the Turks in unspeakable butcheries. The survivors were taken as prisoners and sold in the slave markets of Aleppo. These captives were stripped naked, both men and women, lashed with whips and forced to run before the horses. Those who fell behind were stabbed to death on the way and the roads were covered with Armenian dead bodies.

Female slaves or concubines were kept in the 'harems' for sexual gratification. The codes of conduct of a Moslem vis-à-vis women that we often hear about, are really meant for Moslem women and have nothing to do with a Moslem's behavior with a kafir's wife or mother. Infidel women are beyond the limits set by the holy book. In Islamic societies even a wedded wife is treated as personal property comparable to gold, silver and land. They are veiled and hidden from public view if they happen to be wives. But the concubines are circulated as gifts among the friends.

The afternoon siestas of the Sheikhs of Arab countries and their sexual escapades with slave women or concubines, are common knowledge. If the master, for whatever reason, takes the life of a slave or maims him or her for life, there is no one to question him for the laws of Islam, the 'Sharia' have given the believers unlimited right over the person of the slave.

CHAPTER 14

LOOT AND RAID

Loot and raid in the context of Islam means attacking the kafirs, for a Moslem is not supposed to attack a fellow Moslem. The Arabic word for raid is 'ghazzua' and it also implies killing and enslaving the kafirs. This is the word from which is derived the very honorable term 'ghazi' meaning a warrior of Islam that has killed many kafirs.

The loot taken from the kafir is legal for a Moslem. The distribution of the loot or booty, which includes the men, women and children, is done according to well-defined regulations described in the Koran and the Hadis. The first fifth of the loot goes to the prophet or the caliph and in their absence to the mullah who is in charge. The balance four-fifths are shared by the rest of the fighters who took part in the raid.

In pre-Islamic Arabia, such raids were considered shameful acts. However, the prophet had explained to his followers that since he was the last prophet for all time to come, such raids had now been sanctioned by Allah. Thus the property taken from the kafirs now was quite in order.

CHAPTER 15

ARSON

Arson or burning the property of the kafirs, their houses of worship, their seats of learning, universities and libraries is advised by the Koran. The famous libraries of Alexandria in Egypt, Nalanda in India are notorious examples of arson practised by the followers of Islam. In recent years, the Moslem army of Pakistan resorted to wide-spread arson of Hindu homes in Dacca and other towns of the then East Pakistan, now Bangladesh. Even some Bengali Moslems were not spared for in the eyes of Moslems, anyone who is against him, can be called a kafir and then such barbaric practices get the blessing of the mullah, the representative of Allah. It is common knowledge that the Iranians call the Iraqis, infidels and vice versa. It is truly ingenious how Allah is made to support anything that the believer wants to do for his own satisfaction.

Arson has primarily been used by the Moslems to terrorise the kafirs and weaken them. There is no other inherent quality in such naked destruction of property. Making the kafirs suffer in itself is a holy duty in Islam.

Arson is used frequently by Moslem fundamentalists in countries where they are in a minority. They often burn trains and buses in the streets to show their displeasure with the infidel government of the majority community.

CHAPTER 16

MURDER AND MAYHEM

Murder is an important element in Islam. Murder of the kafirs is of course sacrosanct and approved by the Koran. Murder of the priests of the Kafirs' faith is even more honorable.

In recent times Moslem fanatics have murdered or attempted to murder many religious men of other faiths. Among the Hindus, the famous monks Swami Shraddhananda, Swami Dayananda, Ram Bholey of Mathura, Swami Prakashanandaji of Bangladesh have all been assassinated by Moslem fanatics.

The attempted murder of the Pope is well known. The assailant was a Turk.

Moslems also murder those among themselves who in their opinion are not Islamic enough. Thus we have another set of murders. Mujibur Rahman, Ziaur Rahman, both of Bangladesh, Abdus Samad Khan of India, Liaqat Ali Khan of Pakistan, Anwar Sadat of Egypt, King Abdullah of Jordan, the Liberal P.L.O. leader Sartawi, fall in this category.

The murder of the Sikh Gurus by the Moslem kings of India is also well-known.

When a Moslem murders a kafir, in the eye of Islam no crime has been committed. When, in 1910 A.D., Boutros Pasha was murdered by an Egyptian Moslem for no personal provocation but for the political reason that he had presided over the court that sentenced the Denshawai villagers, and the guilt of the murderer was conclusively proved by evidence, the chief Kazi of Egypt pronounced the judgment that according to Islam it is no crime for a Moslem to slay an unbeliever. Thus we see a criminal like Idi Amin of Uganda getting a safe haven in Saudi Arabia.

There is another kind of murder practised by the followers of Islam. Aurangzib killed his brothers, imprisoned his father, poisoned his own son and nephew, all for the throne really, but Allah's help was beseeched in every case. When an Iraqi kills an Iranian, he is fighting for Islam, for in his eyes the Iranian is an infidel.

Chopping off of limbs, skinning someone alive, gouging the eyes out or pulling out the tongue are very much practised in Islamic countries. If the incidence of meting out such punishment is a little reduced today, that is entirely due to the public opinion in non-Moslem countries. Any criticism of such barbaric acts is often taken as undue interference by kafirs in the internal affairs of an Islamic state.

The assassination of Robert Kennedy, the Jewish athletes in Munich, etc are common knowledge. Terrorism and Islam seem to go so well together.

CHAPTER 17

SOME SPECIAL ASPECTS OF ISLAM

a)   'JIZIYA' OR POLL TAX

All non-Moslems living in an Islamic state is supposed to pay the 'jiziya' or poll tax for the privilege of being there. It was first imposed by Mohammed who bade his followers "fight those who do not profess the true faith, till they pay the 'jiziya' with the hand of humility" (The Koran: IX/29). The books on Moslem Canon Law lay down that the tax has to be paid by the 'zimmi' or kafir allowed to live in the Islamic land, personally. If the 'zimmi' sends the money by an agent, the payment will be refused. The 'zimmi' must come on foot and make the payment standing, while the Moslem receiver should be seated and after placing his hand above that of the 'zimmi' should take the money and cry out, "Oh, 'zimmi'!   pay the commutation money."

The 'zimmis' are those that agree to pay the 'jiziya' and are allowed to live and work in the Islamic land under the following 20 disabilities:

1   They are not to build any new places of worship;

2   They are not to repair any old places of worship which have been destroyed by the Moslems;

3   They are not to prevent Moslem travelers from staying in their places of worship;

4   They are to entertain for three days any Moslem who wants to stay in their homes, and for a longer period if the Moslem falls ill;

5   They are not to harbor any hostility or give aid and comfort to hostile elements;

6   They are not to prevent anyone of them from getting converted to Islam;

7   They have to show respect to every Moslem;

8   They have to allow Moslems to participate in their private meetings;

9   They are not to dress like Moslems;

10   They are not to name themselves with Moslems names;

11   They are not to ride on horses with saddle and bridle;

12   They are not to possess arms;

13   They are not to wear signet rings or seals on their fingers;

14   They are not to sell or drink liquor openly;

15   They are to wear a distinctive dress which shows their inferior status and separates them from the Moslems;

16   They are not to propagate their customs and usages among the Moslems;

17   They are not to build their houses in the neighborhood of Moslems;

18   They are not to bring their dead near the graveyards of the Moslems;

19   They are not to observe their religious practices publicly or mourn their dead loudly;

20   They are not to buy Moslem slaves.

If there are some similarities between the above disabilities and those prescribed by the Nazis for the Jews then the reason is the similarity of motivation. In both cases a section of the population was or is intent on insulting the other section. There is quite an affinity between the Nazi Party Manifesto and the Koran in this respect. The only difference lies in the fact that the Nazi Party Manifesto is a mere political handbook while the Koran claims to be the holy book of a religion supposed to lift up the souls of the followers.

The important expression is 'with the hand of humility'. It is thus that insult was heaped upon the kafir. During the Mughal rule, the Hindus were shaved by Moslem barbers by washing their heads not with water but with urine before applying the razor.

The law of Islam also prescribes death penalty for those who:

1   question the exclusive claims of Islam and its prophet. Those who question the prophet, would be beheaded and those who question the Koran, would have their tongues pulled out;

2   try to revert to their ancestral faith after having once embraced Islam;

3   marry Moslem women without first getting converted into Islam.

The laws of Islam discriminates against the kafirs in matters of testimony in law-courts, taxation and appointment to public offices. This is the reason why one does not see any non-Moslem employees in the higher echelons of the government of Pakistan or Bangladesh. To sum up, the status of a non-Moslem in an Islamic country is that of a hewer of wood or drawer of water. He is subjected to every indignity and pressure to bring him into the fold of Islam.

b)   'JIHAD' OR HOLY WAR

Jihad is a fundamental tenet of Islam like 'kalima', 'namaz', 'hajj', 'rozah' and 'zakaat'[1] .

According to devout Moslems, the best of all prayers in Islam is 'Jihad'. 'Jihad' is the fight that the Moslems of the world would like to wage to bring the whole world under the banner of Islam. Islam wishes to destroy all nations, governments, states anywhere on the face of the earth which are opposed to the ideology and programs of Islam regardless of the country or nation that rules it. The purpose of Islam is to set up a state on the basis of its own ideology. Islam requires the earth - not just a portion, but the whole planet - not because the sovereignty over the earth should be wrested from one nation or several nations and vested in one particular nation, but because the entire mankind should 'benefit' from the ideology and welfare program or what would be truer to say 'Islam' which is the program of 'well-being' for all humanity. THE OBJECTIVE OF JIHAD IS TO ELIMINATE THE RULE OF AN UN-ISLAMIC SYSTEM AND ESTABLISH IN ITS PLACE AN ISLAMIC SYSTEM OF STATE RULE.

Islamic 'Jihad' does not recognise the right of the 'zimmis' to administer state affairs. There are some apologists of 'Jihad' who maintain that the real 'Jihad' in Islam is the fight against one's baser instincts as in Christianity, Buddhism, Judaism and Hinduism. But only a very few people among the Moslems hold such a view and this definition of Islam and 'Jihad' is only a way to mislead the kafirs. The renowned Sufi holy man named Sarmad, who used to practise this kind of spiritual 'Jihad' was executed by the Sunni king Aurangzib. For Aurangzib, the true 'Jihad' was physical war on the kafirs.

c)   POLYGAMY IN ISLAM

A Moslem is permitted to marry four wives at the same time. Islam's apologists say that one should not marry more than one wife if one cannot be sure of being equitable to all four wives. However, it is often the economic factor that regulates the number of wives in a Moslem's life. Even the four wives may not be the same ones all through the life of the Moslem husband. He can divorce his wives by pronouncing the magic word 'talaq' three times. This puts divorce into effect. The wives do not have this privilege.

Once divorced, the husband cannot marry the same divorced wife again unless and until she had been married and divorced in the meantime by another person and the marriage had been consummated.

There is a kind of marriage in Islam which is of predetermined duration. The marriage ends in an automatic divorce at the end of this predetermined period and it is not necessary to pronounce 'talaq' three times. The Shiite Moslems practise such marriage called 'muta' marriage. However, in recent years scores of Sunni Moslems from Saudi Arabia have contracted such marriages with poor Moslem girls of Hyderabad area in India. At the end of the predetermined period, the Indian girls are left by the Saudi 'believers' and the girls, if pregnant have to look after themselves.

Islam does not permit prostitution. However, there is no restriction on a Moslem's having sex with concubines or kafir women. Such women do not have the legal rights of a properly married Moslem wife.

d)   'SHARIAT' IN ISLAM

Islamic Law or 'Shariat' is usually interpreted by the mullahs. Islamic jurisprudence is heavily loaded in favor of the believers. It is therefore futile to expect justice in an Islamic country in a court case between a believer and a non-believer. Non-Moslems have very few rights in an Islamic country. The entire legal system is based not so much on rights but on power and this is true even when the two parties happen to be Moslems. In fact, the Arabic word 'faisalah' meaning 'settle ment' is derived from the Arabic word 'faisal' meaning the 'sword'. Islam's laws are very much based on selective justice.

The laws of Islam do not resemble those of other faiths. A thief is punished by loss of his hand; this is also called 'fore-shortening' of the hand. The first theft makes the thief lose one hand. The second theft takes away a foot from the opposite side of the body. The third theft robs him of the second hand and if he persists, then the other foot goes too. Lashing and stoning to death are common punishments for adultery. Molestation of non-Moslem women by Moslems in an

Islamic country falls outside of the Islamic Laws and no action needs to be taken against the offending party.

Capital punishment is awarded in retaliation for another life that has been taken illegally. It is also awarded for the preservation of the Islamic state. If a kafir kills a Moslem in an Islamic state, no matter for whatever fault on the part of the Moslem, the kafir is executed, unless of course he wants to embrace Islam, to save his life.

During prophet Mohammed's life time, a Jewish woman poet once wrote a few verses against Mohammed as she was embittered by the prophet's treatment of her people. She was assassinated by a Moslem fanatic, a follower of Mohammed, whereupon, Mohammed publicly praised the assassin in the mosque.

Prophet Mohammed had said: "Unmarried man and woman guilty of adultery should be punished with one hundred stripes and one year's banishment. The married couple should be given one hundred stripes and then stoned to death".

However, in spite of the apparent cruelty implied in the punishments, it is often extremely difficult to prove adultery. The 'law' requires that four male 'witnesses' have to answer specific questions on the basis of which the punishment could be administered. The questions are: 1 "What is whoredom?" 2 "In what manner have the parties committed it?" 3 "Where and when?" 4 "With whom?" The four witnesses have to testify that "they have seen the parties in the very act of carnal action."

A distinction exists between sexual intercourse between un-married partners with mutual consent and rape. A Moslem man raping a Moslem woman will have a more serious punish-ment than the 100 lashes and banishment. On the other hand, if a Moslem man rapes a kafir or non-Moslem woman he will not be punished to the same extent. The most that he may have to undergo is a fine depending upon the status of the kafir woman. If a kafir man rapes a Moslem woman, he would be executed often after torture.

Any offense related to property, human body, reputation, Islam, the Islamic state, public peace, decency or morals is treated as criminal offense.

For those who act against the religion of Islam or insult it, the punishments are death, crucifixion, 'fore-shortening' of hands and feet from opposite sides. Letting the accused fall to his death from the top of the minaret of a mosque is another method. 'Fore-shortening' of hands and feet are often done inside a mosque. It is obligatory for all available Moslems to be present to witness the punishments being administered.

In the eye of Islam, even the worst Moslem is better than the best non-Moslem. Maulana Muhammad Ali of India used to say: "According to Islam, even a meanest adulterer Moslem is thousand times better than Mahatma Gandhi".

Islamic Laws are very much feared even by educated Moslems and as a result sometimes they behave in a very shameful and curious manner. Islam forbids music, dancing and painting etc. Fine arts in other cultures are taboo in Islam. In non-Moslem countries the few Moslem artists, film stars or dancers, often change their names to kafir names in public life. In private life they are known by their Moslem names and even practise polygamy, multiple divorces etc. In public life they want to be known as non-Moslems as they are ashamed to dishonor their faith by practising a profession that is specifically forbidden by Allah. In an Islamic country such men and women would have been whipped in public for dancing or taking part in a movie. They however forget that in the Koran it is often said: Allah hears all and sees all. Some say that Islam permits such actions as subterfuges which are tolerated in some cases. How can a Moslem survive otherwise economically in a land of the kafirs and still not dishonor Islam? A little tolerance is called for in such cases and as long as these men and women practise Islamic codes of conduct in their private lives, Allah will forgive them.

e)   'NAMAZ' OR PRAYER

The prayer in Islam is quite different from prayer in other religions. Concentrating the mind, meditation and sitting still to reduce any interference in focussing one's thoughts to the Almighty are not indispensable elements of a Moslem's prayer. He has to pray at certain times of the day, five times in all. He is called upon to pray with others of the same faith. The Friday prayer is very important as it is on Fridays the prophet used to undertake his raids on the kafirs.

There are several body movements in 'Namaz', six in all. He recites or mutters after the mullah who leads the prayer. All praying Moslems are expected to stand up, sit down or bow at the same time. If any non-Moslem procession happens to go by and their festive noises become audible then under the pretext that distraction of the believers' prayer has been caused by the 'unholy' kafirs, the Moslems come out of the mosque and attack the non-Moslems. This 'unholiness' of the kafirs is important for no Moslem has ever protested against similar distraction caused by processions taken out by the Shiite Moslems accompanied by sound of drums and trumpets.

The first prayer takes place early in the morning, while it is still quite dark. The mullah is supposed to go up the minaret and call the followers to prayer in Arabic. But human voice does not go very far and so these days very powerful microphones have been installed on the minarets and the mullah just presses the button and the Arabic chanting comes out of the tape. The petro-dollars have come to the aid of the mullahs all over the world in this enterprise of spreading the message. It is not quite clear how many believers actually get up and attend these prayers at that time of the morning but it surely wakes up a lot of non-believers, disturbing their sleep. In Detroit such activities were stopped by the citizens who protested against this invasion of privacy. To them, one's religion is one's own private affair and it must not be allowed to become a nuisance to others. The fact is that even in Saudi Arabia, the 'namaz' is for servants only, the Sheikhs stay in bed till noon.

f)   'HAREM" OR SERAGLIO

The word 'harem' is derived from the Arabic word 'haram' meaning that which is forbidden. The whole region around Mecca and Medina is 'haram' which implies that things which are allowed elsewhere are forbidden there. This is, of course, due to the inherent 'holiness' and 'inviolate nature' of the regions. It also implies 'forbidden area' and so the word 'harem' implies a sanctuary which is forbidden to the outsiders. This is where the women, both married and unmarried, the slaves and the concubines, live.

No males are allowed inside the 'harem'. Small children born of the women in the 'harem' of course are exempt from this requirement. The women are looked after and also watched by eunuchs. Both white and Negroid eunuchs were extensively used by the Turks. As castration is forbidden in the Koran, the operation was done outside the city without too much publicity. One conveniently forgot that 'Allah knows all and hears all'.

Details of different types of castration in Islamic lands are given in N.M. Penzer's renowned book 'The Harem' published by George G. Harrap & Co Ltd. The kafirs of course could be castrated any time as they do not fall in the category of believers. There were many Abyssinian eunuchs in the 'harems' of Mughal India. Even today, castration is practised in many parts of the Indian subcontinent and most of these eunuchs, surprisingly, are Moslems.

Sir Jadu Nath Sarkar writes in his 'History of Aurangzib': ". . .in the houses of the Delhi nobility luxury was carried to an excess. The 'harems' of many of them were filled with immense numbers of women, of an infinite variety of races, intellect and character. Under Moslem law the sons of concubines are entitled to their patrimony equally with sons born in wedlock, and the children occupy no inferior position in society. Even the sons of lawfully married wives become, at the precocious age, familiar with vice from what they saw and heard in the 'harem', while their mothers were insulted by the higher splendour and influence enjoyed in the same household by younger and fairer rivals of servile origin or easier virtue. THE LOFTY SPIRIT AND MAJESTIC DIGNITY OF A COR-NELIA ARE IMPOSSIBLE IN THE CROWDED HAREM OF A POLYGAMIST; AND WITHOUT CORNELIAS AMONG ⟨THE MOTHERS THERE CANNOT BE GRACCHI AMONG THE SONS."

Footnotes

1.   'Kalima': special incantation to accept Islam;
    'Namaz': prayer;
    'Hajj': pilgrimage to Mecca;
    'Rozah': fasting;
    'Zakaat': charity, alms; money to be used in converting
    non-Moslems or kafirs and also as ransom for the release
    of Moslem prisoners.

CHAPTER 18

THE MULLAH AND THE MOSQUE

The mosque is the house of worship of the Moslems. But unlike the houses of worship of other faiths, it serves quite different purposes as well. Moslem women are generally barred from the usual services in a mosque that women of other faiths perform in their churches, temples, synagogues and gurudwaras. The mosque is often used as a center of administrative and political activities. Sometimes it is used even as an execution ground as well and as a fortress.

Moslem males are required to gather in the mosques for their prayer. Only in exceptional circumstances this rule is waived and prayers allowed in private homes. In the past, when the opposition of the disbelievers took a serious turn, prophet Mohammed himself asked his followers to gather in private homes for prayer. It is for the same reason, in an Islamic country non-Moslems gather in private homes for their worship as the Moslems do not permit them to pray in public or own a church or synagogue or temple for unified prayer.

The prophet Mohammed used his mosque for consultations or important political and military matters and the practice has been continued by his followers till today. On the occasion of the battle of Uhud in which many people died, the prophet had consulted his companions in his mosque after Friday prayers about strategy and planning for the coming confrontation with the enemy.

There have been many cases where the mosque has been used to manufacture arms and to serve as a store-house of weapons. In countries which are considered as 'darul-Harb' or land of war, such practices are encouraged by the mullahs.

95

The mosque is also used as a court-house on some occasions. The Kazi of Medina used to administer justice in the mosque and the practice is followed even today in many places. The practice of using the mosque as a political center was started by the Umayyads. Politics in Islam cannot be dissociated from religion and Islamic politics is quite different from party politics of a parliamentary system. Islamic politics is to strive for the supremacy of the Moslems over the rest of the population and for this purpose any method is acceptable to the mullah. To win over converts or traitors, use of bribes or any other means can be utilised. And once victory is won, the traitors are executed. This has been the way Islam has gained ascendacy in many countries in the past and the method is still being pursued in countries where Moslems are the minority. The mullahs preach their venomous messages inside the mosque to the followers of Islam and keep them from integrating with the national main-stream.

CHAPTER 19

ISLAM AT THE CROSS-ROADS

Islam is a basic religion; some would even call it simplistic. It is a religion of complete surrender and it does not permit asking questions about the dictates of the holy books.

In the past, the Moslems formed a body of people, to whom, spreading the message of Islam by conquest was the accepted way of life. As long as there were fresh lands to conquer, non-Moslem rulers to rebel against, kafirs to plunder, everything went on as usual. Battles were fought, non-Moslem populations subdued and the codes of Islam clamped down.

However, once the conquest was arrested for whatever reason, the Islamic countries found themselves in trouble. Quarrels started between opposing factions. Each side claimed the support of Allah. After the decline of the Arabs, the Turks took over and the caliphate went to the Turks. Some owed allegiance to the Turkish caliph but some did not. Thus, when Aurangzib ascended the throne in India, a powerful country at the time, he called himself the new caliph without paying any attention to the then existing caliphate in Turkey.

The current fight between the Shiites and the Sunnis in the Middle East is a case in point. There are no more Hindus or Sikhs or Christians worth mentioning in Pakistan any more. You cannot attack these non-Moslems for the simple reason that they are not there. It is similar to not being able to have a headache, if the head is missing. But the previously existing unity among the Moslems of different factions seems to have disappeared. Now is the time to fight among themselves. The new object of persecution are the Ahmediyyas, who are being dubbed as non-Moslems. The Shia-Sunni fight in Karachi in recent weeks has taken an ominous turn to the worse.

The real difficulty is caused by the inherent change that our world is subject to. Islam is a rigid religion and no change or improvement is permitted in its practice. The other countries where Islam is not followed, are progressing forward, leaving the Moslems behind. In non-Moslem countries, pursuits in science, arts, education, medicine, physical well-being and intellectual development are being encouraged among men and women alike. But in a Moslem country, it is forbidden for a Moslem woman to be a judge or a lawyer or a ruler and administrator. The world outside seems to get on well with a leader like Britian's Mrs. Thatcher. The United States seems to be quite comfortable with women in the nation's topmost judicial or administrative positions. Several metropolises in America have women mayors; the number of women doctors, nurses, educationists, writers, thinkers and other important professions runs into millions. The progress of women in all non-Islamic countries has been extraordinary in recent years. Scientists like Madame Curie, women astronauts and climbers of the Everest, gymnasts, poets and even executives in big corporations are accepted by non-Moslem societies as a matter of course today. But the Koran is dead against Moslem women undertaking similar responsibilities in Islamic countries.

Although Ghazzali harped on the so-called weaknesses of women, he failed to see the strength that is inherent in the female of the human species. Women who are the mothers of the human race have a tendency to be a great deal more compassionate, tolerant and understanding than average men. The special values of women seem to have been ignored by the proponents of Islam. If the women in Islamic countries are still imprisoned in the 'harem' or its modern equivalent 'the four walls' then the future progress of the Moslem countries is surely going to be negated.

Improvement of the race can only come from freedom and more educated mothers. The mother is the best teacher a child can have. An uneducated or even an educated mother, who lives in an atmosphere of uncertainty of divorce, feels very insecure. This insecurity during his formative years, seeps into the child. He grows up to be a very sad child and eventually takes out his hostilities on others at the slightest pretext, when he grows up and faces the world outside. The extraordinary intolerance, cruelty and selfishness that one comes across in Moslems, may stem from this unhappy child-hood environment which created abnormal personality and behavioral traits passed on by the unhappy mother.

Time has come for the Moslems, in all walks of life, to rectify the situation, regardless of what the mullah says and that includes guys like Khomeini of Iran and Bukhari of India. The alternative is surely going to be as dismal as before. This is an item of social reform that cannot be postponed ad infinitum. The price may be too high, if Moslem women are still left behind in order to propagate the Moslem way of life.

At the same time, the Moslems today must treat the non-Moslems as equals in their own countries. They should have the same rights of propagating their religious systems, cultural values in Islamic countries as the Moslem minorities demand in non-Moslem countries and enjoy. Chasing them away has weakened many Islamic countries. Today the Islamic countries in the Middle East are practically devoid of all other religious minorities due to the intolerance preached by Islam and its followers. The rule of the mullah is supreme and even if a Moslem leader appears who is more liberal than a fanatical fundamentalist, the mullah seems to succeed in getting him out or assassinated. The people do not seem to have any recourse in the matter. The run of the mill Moslem is really very passive in such matters. The Islamic countries are thus denied the special contributions that people of different backgrounds can make. The United States is a good example. Here a Moslem can practise his religion as long as he does not impose it on others by force. But a Christian cannot go to Church in a Moslem country like Kuwait or Saudi Arabia. They cannot decorate their homes on the happy occasion of Christmas. All decorations have to be carefully hidden from public view. Christians have to pray to God in total secrecy and isolation, devoid of community access to sharing their beliefs as brethren. There should be a limit to intolerance! How would the Moslem minorities feel if all non-Moslem countries imposed similar rules against their religion? There are important aspects of judging a nation of people, its religion, and ultimately its sense of morality and relevance to today's world. A great responsibility lies with the Moslems themselves, and if nothing is done soon, then Islam will continue to be synonymous with terrorism, death and bar-barity.

The news report on Pakistan today taken from India's renowned Illustrated Weekly of India dated February 27, 1983 is illustrative of Islam's treatment of its own followers especially the women:

Inside Pakistan Today--1

Women Are Not For Whipping

Strange indeed, are the doings of Pakistan's mullahs, moulvis, and military rulers. The country's new laws have reduced women to helpless targets.

by Lopamudra

For the first time in Pakistan a few weeks ago a woman was publicly whipped at Swat, Peshawar. Her husband had charged her with infidelity. The woman was arrested and a case against her filed under the Islamic Hudood Ordinance by the sessions Judge at Swat. She was sentenced to five years' imprisonment and fined Rs 10,000. Her appeal to the Federal Shariat Court was set aside. That was not all. She was publicly given 20 lashes. Pakistani women organised a Women's Action Forum against this "cruel game" and voiced their protest to General Zia but to no effect.

Last year in September an 18-year-old girl, Fahmida, was administered 100 whips and her lover, Allah Bux, a bus driver, was sentenced to be stoned to death publicly. This sentence is, however, yet to be carried out.

Fahmida, a Std X student of the Prince Karim Aga Khan School, had produced papers of her marriage to the driver, which were rejected on the ground that at the time of marriage she was pregnant.

Eight prominent women's organisations in Karachi formed a Women's Action Forum, collected signatures against the Shariat order and sent them to general Zia. Fahmida's sentence was suspended till the disposal of her appeal in the Shariat Court, but it is feared that, after Swat, it may fare no better.

Not content with corporal punishment, the mullahs continue to heap atrocities on hapless women. In October, a new-born child was stoned to death near a mosque in Karachi. A mullah on seeing a crying child on the stairs of the mosque, gave the 'fatwa' (without making any inquiry) that the child was illegitimate, and should be stoned to death. The first stone was thrown by the mullah himself. Thereafter a mad crowd showered the child with stones. When a few passers by tried to save it, they too were injured. The daily 'Dawn' further stated that witnesses were threatened with dire consequences if the news was leaked to the press. Fortunately, however, the press 'did' get the information.

Strange are the doings of such mullahs, moulvis and military rulers. Dr. Asrar Ahmed, one of the leading religious scholars, has petitioned the 'Majlis-e-Shoora' (Federal Council) that since women are responsible for the growing rise in sex crimes they should not be appointed to Government posts or selected for the 'Majlis-e-Shoora' and other institutions, but confined to their homes.

It is also proposed to reduce the marriageable age for girls in Pakistan under the Islamic law from 18 to 15. Besides, a demand has been tabled in the Federal Council to rescind the Family Law Ordinance which says that a man cannot marry a second time without the first wife's permission.

The Woman's Value

General Zia has further issued a law which fixes a woman's value as half that of a man's. According to this law, if a man is murdered, the victim's next of kin can demand either the death of the murderer or accept in lieu of it 4.36 kg of gold as compensation. If the victim is a woman, only half this quantity of gold is to be paid.

There is also a strong movement all over Pakistan for keeping women in 'purdah'. Yet another indignity is an order instructing female TV announcers to keep their heads covered. In fact, a popular TV announcer was sacked for failing to comply with it. The mullahs propound a ridiculous justification. If women remain bare-headed, they emit rays that harm men.

An inevitable consequence of these harsh rules (of confining women within the four walls of their homes) is the phenomenon of kidnapping. Even worse is the actual sale of girls by their parents, another common occurrence.

Not only is crime against women in Pakistan on the rise, with an ever-increasing number of rape incidents and wife-burning, but it is only the women who are the helpless targets of new laws.

Only recently a lawyer, Ansari Barri, had filed a petition in Pakistan's Federal Shariat Court that women's appointment to the posts of judges, etc, should be declared illegal. Fortunately, the full bench of the Federal Shariat Court gave a decision that it is not against Islam to appoint women as kazis, judges and magistrates.

Though the women have won this battle, there is no end to the prejudices against them. Two separate medical colleges have been opened for women. But according to a prominent teacher, Anita Gulam Ali, the girls grduating from these colleges will get fewer opportunities than men to further their career.

At present only 11 per cent of the total population of women in Pakistan is literate. Of the 65 lakh school-going children, only 20 lakh are girls.

Women doctors, lawyers, professors, judges etc. are being continually discouraged from providing serious competition to their male counterparts. In the same strain, women athletes have been forbidden to participate in international sports competitions, the Asiad being the most recent example.

A WORD OF CAUTION TO THE KAFIR HINDU

Many Hindus in their eagerness to emphasise that there is no fundamental difference between a practising Moslem and a Hindu, often overstep certain limits without realizing an important fact. In India, it is common practice to mention that the Moslems of India (who had been crying hoarse for so many years that they belong to a different race because of their Moslem faith and so cannot live together with the Hindus) are really descendants of the same ancestors. These Hindus good-naturedly but foolishly imply that the Moslems are as proud of their common heritage as are the Hindus of India for instance.

Not knowing the make-up of the mind of a practising Moslem, these Hindus forget the fact that in Islam, anything that had existed before the acceptance of the prophet's faith is considered the remnant of the Dark Age or 'jahiliya'. For a converted Moslem or a Moslem whose ancestors were converted several generations ago, his ancient Hindu roots are not a subject of pride. He feels insulted when a Hindu tries to equate him with his pre-Islamic ancestors, and thereby derives some sort of a satisfaction by implying that they, the Moslem and the Hindu, are more or less of the same category in the context of the nation at large. The Hindu does not realize that the Hindu heritage of India is a shameful thing to his Moslem compatriot. It always has been and is going to be that way as long as the Koran's injunctions are obeyed by the faithful.

It is practically impossible for the two communities to mix and mingle as normal people do. The Moslems keep their women away from other males while a Hindu, a Sikh or a Christian attends social gatherings together with their women-folk. You never find a 'true' non-Moslem friend for a practising Moslem. And this is true for any country, where

people of different faiths live together. The Koran's injunctions are quite clear on the subject. It forbids a Moslem to
make friends with the infidels. That they belong to the same
country is not so important. For a Moslem of India, a Saudi
Moslem who is an alien in the common international parlance,
is nearer to him than the Hindu or Christian who lives next
door.

The inherent separatism preached by Islam is a point
that many kafirs lose sight of and come to regret later.
Barring a few exceptions, the great majority of Moslems do
not consider themselves part of the national mainstream, if
the country happens to be a 'darul-Harb'. It does not matter
how many high positions are offered to the Moslems as a
gesture of good-will, in his mind he considers himself quite
separate from the unbelievers. In a darul-Islam like Pakistan
or Bangladesh for instance, one does not see any Hindu or
Christian people at high level jobs, be it in the administration,
the foreign service, the army, navy or air force. Invariably,
the difference in the two attitudes comes to be realized by the
non-Moslems much too late to their chagrin. There was a
reason for Pakistan being created and the same forces are still
in operation in the rest of India as in Lebanon. There are
people who compare Pakistan and Bangladesh as safe deposit
accounts for the Islamics while secular India is a kind of joint
account where the Moslems share the wealth of the country
along with the rest of the population. Pakistan and Bangladesh
of course prevent the non-Moslem population of these
countries all rights of becoming citizens.

William K. Stevens of NY Times wrote recently:

> "When the Roman Empire was dying and much classical
> learning lay in ashes, and the Dark Ages were descending
> on the West, there flourished on the plains of northern
> India not only the most civilized culture of its time, but
> also one of the most creative in history.

> "There, under the Gupta emperors, 1000 years before
> Galileo and Kepler and Newton, Indian thinkers develop-
> ed a revolutionary idea without which modern science
> could not exist: the concept of mathematical zero,
> along with the related system of numerals that is called

Arabic but was, in fact, invented here. By the fifth century, an Indian had discovered the Earth's axial rotation. Well before the Renaissance re-illuminated Europe, Indian mathematicians had explored the upland realms of quadratic equations and cube roots, had become the first to assign 3.1416 as the value of 'pi', and had mastered the concept of infinity. Throughout most of history, in fact, Indian science and Indian culture generally matched and at times exceeded anything anywhere else in the world".

The advent of the Moslem hordes from west Asia, and their concept of 'jahiliya' combined with the Hindus' misplaced humanitarian attitude toward the invaders greatly damaged this civilization of the kafirs.

The Hindus of India should be aware of the three principal sources of danger that can come from the Islamic ideology, an ideology that does not recognize the existence of any other faith or culture on this earth.

DANGER 1:

This of course is the usual battle and direct confrontation with the invader. The kafir has defeated the Moslem many times but not having known the nature of his adversary, let him go after defeating him. The Moslem came back with heavier and heavier reinforcement and if the kafir lost a single battle, then that was the end of him, and often the end of his people and dynasty. The kafir's negligence in delivering proper retribution made him pay dearly. History is a residual chronicle of such incidents.

DANGER 2:

When the Moslem found that the attitude of the kafir had hardened, he had recourse to subterfuge. To soften up the kafir's attitude toward Islam, a new sect, the Sufis were created. The decision to create this sect was first taken in a secret religious meeting in Baghdad in the year 1180 A.D. The idea was to show the kafirs the gentler side of Islam. The Sufis adopted many of the religious tenets of the kafirs such as tolerance, compassion and charity to all instead of being selective as in Islam. The Sufis did succeed considerably in the enterprise and the Hindus became the disciples of these Sufis in great numbers. In many instances, a Sufi had more Hindu followers than Moslems.

The main body of the Moslems did not accept the Sufis as their religious leaders. However, for 'other reasons' they were tolerated by the Moslem king or 'amir-ul-mominin'. In the case of the fundamentalist kings like Aurangzib, this did not work out. Aurangzib executed the renowned Sufi Sarmad during his reign.

When the time for final onslaught came, the Sufis were no where to be found. Behold! They were on the side of the Moslem attackers who were being directed by the Sufi holymen themselves, along with the usual fire-belching mullahs that accompanied the invaders. The Sufis showed the invaders the places to loot, edifices to destroy, and any secret hiding places that the kafirs might have. This in the end, and at great sacrifice, opened the eyes of the kafirs and the influence of the Sufis among the kafirs dwindled. But by then great chunks of the kafir territory had been annexed by the Moslems.

DANGER 3:

Of all three, this is the most dangerous source of turmoil.

There is a breed of kafir leaders who claim to represent the interests of the kafirs, but in reality they look after their own interests as well as the interests of the Moslems, letting down the kafirs every time. Mahatma Gandhi and Pandit Nehru were such leaders. India's current prime minister Indira Gandhi is another example.

Mahatma Gandhi was born and brought up among the Moslems of Gujarat[1] . His entire education from schools in India to Law college in London was paid for by his Moslem guardian. His business in South Africa was also established at the Moslem's expense. Gandhi was hired by a wealthy Moslem businessman in South Africa. His entire educational life was spent living among the Moslems. In London, he was part of the Anjumane Islamiah which later developed into Muslim League. His knowledge of Hindu scriptures was superficial at best.

In order to bring the Hindus and the Moslems together, Gandhi used to introduce Islamic tenets into Hindu prayers. The Moslems hardly attended his prayers and refused out of hand any such mixing of the two religions in his prayers. In one of his post-prayer speeches delivered on 6th April, 1947 (the year India was partitioned), he said: "Hindus should never be angry against the Moslems, even if the latter might make up their mind to undo even their existence. If they put all of us to the sword, we should court death bravely. We should never fear death. We are destined to be born and die; why should we feel gloomy over it? If all of us die with a smile on our lips, we shall enter a new life. We shall originate a new Hindusthan."

Gandhi supported the Khilafat movement. It must be recalled that the Khilafat (or Caliphate of the Turkish king, after the first world war) was totally unworthy of support of the progressive Moslems. Kemal Ataturk established this fact by abolition of the Khilafat. The abolition of the Khilafat was widely welcomed by enlightened Moslem opinion the world over and Kemal was the undoubted hero of all young Moslems fighting against Imperial domination. But Gandhi used to frequent the most fanatic type of Moslems and he gave his full support to this movement. The apostle of non-violence sent an invitation to the king of Afghanistan to attack India to rid the country of all kafirs. Gandhi was ignorant of the fact that the first four Caliphs were the real ones and the rest were spurious.

The forcible conversion of Hindus was happening all over India at this time, and for the first time a Hindu monk came up reconverting them back to Hinduism, a deed that was neglected by the Hindu religious leaders for many years. The name of this monk was Swami Shraddhananda. The Moslems could not tolerate this kind of re-conversion and one day one Moslem young man, one Abdul Rashid murdered the monk. The Moslems all over the country were jubilant. One Asaf Ali came forward to defend the assassin but his guilt was established and Abdul Rashid was hanged by the British. Later, Pandit Nehru hired this Asaf Ali as India's ambassador to the United States.

Mahatma Gandhi, who had not assented to put his signature to a petition for saving the lives of great patriots like Bhagat Singh and others, because they took part in violence, and had also for the same reason called Shivaji, Rana Pratap and Guru Gobind Singh, all Hindu heroes, as 'misguided patriots', did not however, look upon Rashid's act in that light. No one had ever heard Mr. Gandhi denounce the acts of bigotry of Aurangzib or Shah Jahan either.

Gandhi took the murderer Suhrawardy under his wings when Suhrawardy was sought by the young men of Bengal to avenge the gruesome murder of Haren Ghosh (see page 64).

Gandhi gave his full support to Ali Brothers who had more than once affirmed their loyalty to the doctrine of Pan-Islamism.

Mahatma Gandhi's sayings in the wake of the Moplah[2] riots in Kerala are noteworthy. Moplahs had originally rebelled against the British but the British repressed them savagely. Moplahs, defeated and frustrated, now turned their wrath against the unsuspecting Hindus; for the Hindus, in their eyes were as much kafirs as the British. The Hindu who had lost himself in chanting 'Hindu Muslim Bhai Bhai' (Hindus and Moslems are brothers), was attacked by the Moslem chanting 'Allahu-Akbar' (Allah is great, the battle cry against the kafirs). The number of Hindus murdered was 3000; the number of those forcibly converted, over 20,000 and property looted about Rs30 million. There was no end to molestations and abductions of Hindu women.

Dr. Annie Besant stated: "They murdered and plundered abundantly, and killed or drove all Hindus who would not apostatize. Somewhere about one hundred thousand people were driven from their homes with nothing but the clothes they had on, stripped of everything. . .Malabar has taught us what Islamic rule still means, and we do not want to see another specimen of the Khilafat Raj in India. How sympathy with the Moplahs is felt by the Muslims outside Malabar has been proved by the defense raised by them for their fellow believers, and by Mr. Gandhi himself, who stated that they had acted as they believed that religion taught them to act. I felt that this is true; but there is no place in a civilized land for people who drive away out of the country those who refuse to apostatize from their ancestral faiths."

In reference to Moplah rioters, Gandhi said: "They are a brave God-fearing people who were fighting for what they consider as religion, and in a manner which they considered religious."

Gandhi had assured all Indians at the time of partition that India could only be divided over his dead body. The gullible kafirs found him still alive and well although the country was divided and millions murdered in the process.

Gandhi's Islamic upbringing, however, was clearly evident in his sexual aberrations. He used to sleep with multiple women, mostly very young, completely nude. The practice was kept a secret for a long time but finally was found out at the Sabaramati Ashram. He gave up beating his wife Kasturba only on his arrival in India. Gandhi practised the Islamic tenet of beating the wife on a regular basis when he was in South Africa.

The upbringing of Pandit Nehru was entirely Islamic and he was proud of the fact. His name Jawaharlal Nehru was Persian and Islamic. He used to boast that he was culturally Islamic and a Hindu only by accident. He used this accidental fact over and over again as his claim to the leadership of the Hindus in his encounters with the Muslim League led by Mohammed Ali Jinnah and every time he let the Hindus down.

Once after the country was divided and an orgy of murder, arson and rape was continuing on the Pakistani side of the border and Hindu and Sikh refugees were streaming in, the Pandit declared over the radio that all refugees should forgive the Moslems for all that the Moslems had done to them and not think of revenge. The radio broadcast was heard in all refugee camps in Delhi, Amritsar, Ludhiana, Jullunder, etc. Next morning, Nehru accompanied by Indira Gandhi, his daughter went to visit one of the camps. Indira Gandhi was just behind Pandit Nehru and a very old man, an octogenarian, touched the hand of Indira Gandhi, a girl of his granddaughter's age. Nehru flared up and slapped the old man, an eminent businessman from Lahore, who was now a pauper.

Instead of getting angry, the old man laughed out loud to Nehru's face and said: "You spoke over the radio last night and advised us not to be revengeful but forgiving toward the Moslems. Your daughter is like my grand-daughter; you yourself are like my son in age. What did I do wrong in touching the hand of your daughter to attract your attention? You flew into a rage and slapped me! And you advised me over the radio to calm my anger? Do you know, three of my daughters were taken away by force by the Moslems from my home and I should not be angry? What gives you the right to slap me just for touching your daughter?" The Moslem-loving Pandit moved away like a dog with his tail between his legs.

The Hindus 'must' avoid choosing false leaders. Leaders who make use of their political position to advertise their own idiosyncrasies are not good leaders. Morarji Desai was one such leader who advertised his urine therapy as soon as he became India's prime minister. Until then, he had never mentioned it. One wonders what prime ministership has got to do with urine therapy? Some think that Gandhi, Nehru and Desai behaved in such shameful way in order to get recognition from the public.

Aurangzib used to destroy the Hindus' houses of worship, their schools and libraries with the help of his army. Nehru did the same in a much more refined way. When the Nagarjunsagara Dam was completed and it was going to be filled up with water, Nehru at the advice of some of his Moslem secretaries, raised the level of water much above the level initially fixed by the engineers. This was done to drown a lot more Hindu temples than were originally estimated. He had no empathy for the ancient heritage of the Hindus having been brought up in Islamic atmosphere himself. He read about the ancient glory of the Hindu civilization in later years and used to boast of having discovered India himself in his late life.

Nehru gave away an Indian enclave to Pakistan without first getting the approval of the Indian Parliament[3]. When the Pakistanis attacked India without any provocation and India sustained heavy losses, Nehru threw in Hindu and Sikh soldiers to protect the Moslem inhabitants of Kashmir from the attack of the invaders. Eventually, the Indian army pushed back the Pakistanis and just when the Indian army was to launch a punishing attack on the Moslems, Nehru stopped the Indians and went to settle the dispute to the United Nations Assembly. Since then, the problem has lingered and Nehru succeeded in getting the Hindus in a situation that no pandit[4] worth his name should have done.

Pandit Nehru's fraternising with the Moslems was phenomenal. In fact, people used to say that in the whole of India, there was only one nationalist Moslem and that was Pandit Nehru. The implication was that the real Moslems were NOT nationalists but fundamentalists, who were Moslems first and Indians second.

Indira Gandhi, the current prime miniter has also more Moslem family friends than Hindus. She hates to be identified with the Hindus on whose support she has become the prime minister. She had once declared that she would hate to have a Hindu as her husband. It is only for political reasons that of late she has started visiting Hindu temples. Her son Sanjay Gandhi (alias Sanjeev) was circumcised like a Moslem child [5] .

When the 90,000 Pakistani soldiers surrendered to the kafir army of India, Indira Gandhi fed these ruffians and lodged and clothed them, for months, instead of trying them for having killed innocent kafirs in East Pakistan, raping their women and burning their homes, nearly three million of them. She did not bring any charge against the captured soldiers and their generals. Everyone was released and let go back to Pakistan scot free while the Hindu and Sikh soldiers that Pakistan had captured, were mostly murdered by Pakistan in the prison camps and very few were returned.

Indira Gandhi allowed Moslem infiltrators to come to India from Bangladesh and gave them citizenship papers while the bonafide Hindu refugees from Islamic Bangladesh did not receive any welcome. Her treatment of the Hindu refugees leaves much to be desired. This is in stark contrast with the treatment of Moslems who had left India at the time of partition but came back later. These turn-coats were welcomed with open arms in Kashmir and elsewhere.

Another Moslem gentlemen, who was a family friend of the Nehrus, was one Syud Husain. He had once eloped with Indira's aunt Vijay Lakshmi Pandit, who later occupied the highest post of the United Nations. This Syud Husain was later hired by Nehru in the Indian Foreign Service and made India's ambassador to Egypt. When he died, the government of India erected a mausoleum in his honor in Cairo. On the other hand, not even a small brick pillar has been built by the Nehru or Gandhi government of India for the three million kafirs murdered in East and West Pakistans by the Moslems of West Pakistan.

Consider the case of the 50 new mosques which currently are being built in one of the holiest Hindu cities of India, Mathura. It is here that the Krishna temple was destroyed so many times by Aurangzib and Ahmed Shah Abdali. Hindus have rebuilt the temple at an adjacent place, as the old foundation could not be built upon, the Moslems having built a mosque on the old emplacement. The mosque could have been destroyed by the Hindus too as it is a Hindu city and very few Moslems live there today. But the Hindus did not do that. They left the mosque in peace and built a new Krishna temple near the old site.

The other day Rukmini Arundale met Mrs. Gandhi. She had two requests to make to the P.M. She said that the government of India should assess the Saudi money entering the country to subvert Hindu culture. She also asked the P.M. to find out if Saudi petrodollars were financing the construction of fifty new mosques in Mathura. The P.M. was not even aware of these goings on and a quick inquiry revealed that it was indeed a fact that the Saudis were financing mosque building in Mathura.

Now, the fact is that the mosque once built by Aurangzib remains mostly unattended in Mathura. There are not too many Moslems in this heavily populated Hindu city. What are the Moslems going to do with not one but fifty new mosques there?

But from the nuisance point of view these mosques can create a lot of trouble. The Moslems are supposed to pray five times a day and thus five times fifty or two hundred and fifty times a day, the powerful microphones will blare out the Arabic chantings, creating a lot of bad blood and invading the privacy of the Hindu pilgrims. The tolerance of the kafirs is being stretched a little too far by the P.M. of India. Just to think that a kafir cannot even travel to Mecca, not to speak of building fifty or even one temple or church or synagogue there and the prime minister of India is not even aware of the serious enterprise in Mathura that is calculated to disturb the peace in a Hindu holy city! Can things become worse than that? This behavior of the current P.M. of India is due to her Islamic upbringing. A lot of harm will come to the kafirs of India from this source alone, if they are not careful.

Indira Gandhi promoted a Kashmiri Moslem to the post of India's ambassador and a cabinet minister whose capabilities can well be described by his propensity to procure prostitutes in Europe at the expense of the Indian taxpayers. This Moslem gentlemen used to draw 100 Swiss francs from the entertainment account every day for a prostitute when the late N. Gopalaswamy Ayyangar went to attend the Kashmir meeting in Geneva. If only poor Indians knew how their hard-earned money was being spent by a Moslem under the patronage of Mrs. Gandhi; and to think that the Koran forbids prostitution![6]

Another source of danger comes from the priests of the kafirs. Many of them, though supposedly priests, do not know the basic fundamentals of the Hindu faith. They have neglected the lower castes of the Hindus and often subscribed to their persecution for ages.

Many of these priests are paid money to lend their services to undertake enterprises calculated to erode the Hindu society. Rama Krishna Math of Madras is one such organisation. For money received from the government of India, this organisation publishes and distributes the teachings of the Koran to the Hindus and other kafirs. The teachings are misleading and written up to resemble Hindu teachings. The book entitled 'Thus Spake Prophet Muhammad' published by the Rama Krishna Math does NOT present the true injunctions of the Koran that refer to the kafirs. The book has been presented as a benign book, preaching precepts that are similar to the techings of the Buddha, Lord Krishna and other Hindu incarnations.

Perhaps the most surprising thing, is that none of these Hindu kafir monks have read the Koran but glibly proclaim that Islam preaches the same kind of message that one receives from the Bible or the Tripitaka (the holy book of the Buddhists) or the Vedas of the Hindus. Most of these monks 'pretend' to have read the Islamic holy books. In reality they are too lazy to delve into Allah's injunctions for if they did, they would have found out that the first thing Allah wants is to decimate these priests who have placed rivals of Allah for their worship. In fact, these Hindu kafir monks are really cheating their community and misguiding the Hindu kafirs who listen to them.

The Moslems like everyone else respect the strong. The saying goes: "Mushalam manati yah sah Mushalmanah asti" which means that Moslem respects the clout or 'mushalam' and so he is called a 'mushalman'.

Nehru and Mahatma Gandhi failed to be strong with the Moslems. They were incapable of planning wisely, daring boldly and achieving strenuously or of wresting victory from the jaws of defeat by desperate effort or heroic endurance. Whenever the going got tough, Nehru went to Lord Mountbatten or to the United Nations and Gandhi fasted. In spite of a few dams and steel mills which were built by the foreigners anyway like the movie "Gandhi", the fact remains that Nehru and Gandhi together have saddled India's kafirs with unnecessary problems which of course they have to solve now by themselves. The mitigating factor, is the absence of these two 'holier than thou' politicians. That, itself might make matters easier.

Swami Vivekananda had said: "For instance, the Mohammedan religion allows Mohammedans to kill all who are not of their religion. It is clearly stated in the Koran. "Kill the infidels if they do not become Mohammedans." They must be put to fire and sword. Now if you tell a Mohammedan that this is wrong, he will naturally ask. "How do you know that? How do you know it is not good? My book says it is." You say your book is older; there will come the Buddhist, and say, my book is much older still. Then will come the Hindu, and say, my books are the oldest of all. Therefore, referring to books will not do. . .

"No amount of books can help us to become purer. The only power is in realisation, and that lies in ourselves and comes from thinking. Let me think. A clod of earth never thinks; but it remains only a lump of earth. The glory of man is that he is a thinking being. It is the nature of man to think and therein he differs from animals. I believe in reason, having seen enough of the evils of authority, for I was born in a country where they have gone to the extreme of authority."

It is therefore extremely important for the kafirs to learn about Islam and its attitude toward them. Any attempt to protect the life, limb, culture, and property of the kafirs should start from an adequate knowledge of the edicts of Islam. Thus knowledge of the Koran is very important to the kafir, not only as a source of general knowledge but also as a means for survival.

There are strong indications that the Moslem countries of west Asia have laid a deep-seated plot to Islamise India before the Hindus and other non-Moslems of the subcontinent wake up to the fact. The half-Islamised current rulers of India and some misguided Hindu religious organisations are at work to help the Moslem Arabs in their sinister enterprise. The Moslem residents of India, who overnight have become champions of secularism, are like a dagger poised at the heart of the darul-Harb, that is India. Time for action and organisation has come.

Footnotes

1. Some say that Gandhi's natural father was the Moslem employer of Gandhi's father. Gandhi's father used to work for a Moslem landowner and had stolen money from the cash box and had fled. He was a fugitive for three years and his wife was taken over by the Moslem landlord and placed in his harem. Gandhi was born during this period when his father was a fugitive. There are people who assert that Gandhi's father used to come inside the harem like a thief to sleep with his wife, and he indeed was the true father but that seems to be highly unlikely. However! Gandhi had promised to his mother to be a strict vegetarian. This promise he kept all throughout his life. Otherwise he was a servant of Islam in his political dealings.

2. Moplahs are Moslems from the Malabar area in Kerala, South India.

3. Berubari was ceded to East Pakistan without previously asking the opinion of the residents of Berubari.

4. Pandit; a learned man.

5. Dark thoughts cross many minds at the uncanny likeness of Sanjay with one Mohammed Yunus, a family friend of the Nehrus. Like Yunus, Sanjay too had a hot temper and inclination toward breaking the law. Sanjay had a clash with the British law and he changed his name from Sanjeev to Sanjay then to get out of the law's reach. A son of Yunus (Shahriyar by name) is still serving sentence in a US prison. Sanjay had a balding pate like Yunus has. The other brother, Rajiv is of an entirely different disposition and physical appearance. Sanjay's marriage took place in the house of Mohammed Yunus and at Sanjay's death, Yunus displayed publicly his uncontrollable grief when he sobbed and wept relentlessly.

6. The Moslem diplomat's name is Mohammed Shafi Qureshi. Qureshi is an honorable name is Islam.

CHAPTER 21

A SHORT LIFE SKETCH OF MOHAMMED

Mohammed was born in the year 570 A.D. His father had died a few months before his birth. He lost his mother when he was about six years of age. Mohammed was brought up by his uncle.

Financially Mohammed was very poor. Some say that Mohammed was illiterate but opinions differ on this. Education or no education, Mohammed was very intelligent and wise. He was thoughtful and meditative.

It is said that Mohammed was of medium build and not too tall or short. Since no formal pictures of Mohammed are available, one has to go by descriptions of Mohammed written by his followers. Mohammed was handsome, had a large head with black thick hair, wide forehead, heavy eyebrows and large black eyes with slight redness on the sides and long eyelashes. He had a fine nose, well spaced teeth and a thick beard, wide chest and shoulders, light colored skin and thick palms and feet.

Mohammed was married by Khadija Bibi, his employer and 15 years his senior. At the time, Mohammed was twenty-five years old. Mohammed was Khadija Bibi's third husband; the lady was a widow when she married Mohammed.

Khadija Bibi was wealthy and after marriage with her, Mohammed lived in comparative luxury, for the first time in his life. They had several children, both boys and girls. The boys did not live long and the girls were given away in marriage. They adopted a son named Zayed after their sons died.

Khadija Bibi died when Mohammed was about 49 years old. Between the ages of 49 and 63, after Khadija died, the prophet married thirteen wives. The names of eleven are given below. At the age of 54 Mohammed married Ayesha, a girl of six (some say nine) years of age. Ayesha was the daughter of Abu Bakr, a close disciple of Mohammed. Ayesha, according to many was Mohammed's most favorite wife.

Mohammed's Wives:
1   Khadija Bibi
2   Sauda Bibi
3   Ayesha Bibi
4   Hafsa Bibi
5   Umme-Habiba Bibi
6   Umme-Salma Bibi
7   Safia Bibi
8   Moyumuna Bibi
9   Zainab bint Jahsh Bibi
10   Zainab bint Khuzaymah Bibi
11   Juwairya (Zudia) Bibi

Zainab, daughter of Jahsh was initially married to his adopted son Zayed. But one day the prophet 'beheld in a loose undress, the beauty of Zainab, and burst forth into an ejaculation of devotion and desire. The servile, or grateful, freeman understood the hint, and yielded without hesitation to the love of the benefactor'. Zayed divorced Zainab so that Mohammed could marry her.

Among Mohammed's concubines were Rehana and Mary (also known as Mariam). Mary was a Christian slave girl presented to Mohammed whereas Juwairya and Rehana both were Jewish girls captured in battles with the Jews. Juwairya eventually married the prophet and gave up her Jewish faith. Rehana did not agree to give up her Jewish faith and would rather live as a concubine against her own will, than marry the prophet. Both Juwairya and Rehana had lost their men folk in the battles with the Moslem followers of Mohammed.

Among the many battles that the prophet of Islam fought with his enemies, the kafirs, the more wellknown are the following:

Battle of Badr: the Qurayza were defeated. (624 A.D.)

Battle of Uhud: the Moslems were defeated. (625 A.D.)

War of the ditch: Meccans attack the Moslems and the attackers are driven off. (627 A.D.)

Battle of Khaybar: the Jews are defeated. (629 A.D.)

In the year 627 A.D. the Jewish tribe of Qurayza was raided by Mohammed. Some 700 men were beheaded. Edward Gibbon writes in his famous book, 'The Decline and Fall of the Roman Empire': ". . .seven hundred Jews ere dragged in chains to the market-place of the city; they descended alive into the grave prepared for their execution and burial; and the apostle beheld with an inflexible eye the slaughter of his helpless enemies.   Their sheep and camels were inherited by the Musulmans: three hundred cuirasses, five hundred pikes, a thousand lances, composed the most useful portion of the spoil."

All the Jews that survived the battle of Khaybar were also put to the sword in 629 A.D.

It was in 630 A.D. that Mecca was taken by Mohammed. The entire population was converted to Islam and the Kaaba established as the religious center of Islam. All kafirs were forbidden entry into Mecca.

The Moslem year starts from 622 A.D. This is the year of HIJRA or flight of Mohammed and his followers to Medina.

Mohammed believed that he was poisoned by a Jewish woman as revenge after the battle of Khaybar. During the last four years of his life, his health declined, epileptic fits became more frequent, his other infirmities increased.   He died in the year 632 A.D., June 8.

During the twenty-four years of his marriage with Khadija Bibi, the youthful prophet abstained from the right of polygamy and just before his impending death he liberated his slaves: seventeen men and eleven women. Till the third day before his death he regularly performed the function of public prayer.   Gibbon says in his book: "In spite of his polygamy Mohammed left no heir. In 655 or 656 A.D. his son in law, Ali, became Commander of the Faithful, but his descendants did not retain power".

APPENDIX 1

(By Sir Jadu Nath Sarkar)

TEMPLE DESTRUCTION BY AURANGZIB

BEFORE ACCESSION.

"The temple of Chintaman, situated close to Sarashpur, and built by Sitadas jeweller, was converted into a mosque named 'Quwat-ul-Islam' by order of the Prince Aurangzib, in 1645," (Mirat-i-Ahmadi, 232.) The 'Bombay Gazetteer', vol. 1. pt. 1. p. 280, adds that he slaughtered a cow in the temple, but Shah Jahan ordered the building to be restored to the Hindus.

"In Ahmadabad and other 'parganas' of Gujrat in the days before my accession (many) temples were destroyed by my order. They have been repaired and idol worship has been resumed. Carry out the former order." 'Farman' dated 20 Nov., 1665. (Mirat, 275).

"The village of Satara near Aurangabad was my hunting-ground. Here on the top of the hill stood a temple with an image of Khande Rai. By God's grace I demolished it, and forbade the temple dancers ('murlis') to ply their shameful trade,"--Aurangzib to Bidar Bakht in 'Kalimat-i-Tayyibat, 7b'.

AFTER ACCESSION.

"It has been decided according to our Canon Law that long standing temples should not be demolished, but no new temple allowed to be built... Information has reached our...Court that certain persons have harassed the Hindus resident in Benares and its environs and certain Brahmans who have the right of holding charge of the ancient temples there, and that they further desire to remove these Brahmans from their ancient office. Therefore, our royal command is that you should direct that in future no person shall in unlawful ways interfere with or disturb the Brahmans and other Hindus resident in those places."--Aurangzib's "Benares farman" addressed to Abul Hasan, dated 28th Feb., 1659, granted through the mediation of Prince Muhammad Sultan. J. A. S. B, 1911, p. 689, with many mistakes notably about the date, which I have corrected from a photograph of the 'farman'.

"The temple of Somnath was demolished early in my reign and idol worship (there) put down. It is not known what the state of things there is at present. If the idolators have again taken to the worship of images at the place, then destroy the temple in such a way that no trace of the building may be left, and also expel them (the worshippers) from the place."--Letter of Aurangzib in the last decade of his reign. Inayetullah's 'Ahkam', 10a; Mirat 372.

19 Dec., 1661. Mir Jumla entered the city of Kuch Bihar, which had been evacuated by its king and people, and "appointed Sayyid Md. Sadiq to be chief judge, with directions to destroy all the Hindu temples and to erect mosques in their stead. The general himself with a battle-axe broke the image of Narayan."--Stewart's 'Bengal'.

"The Emperor learning that in the temple of Keshav Rai at Mathura there was a stone railing presented by Dara Shukoh, remarked, 'In the Muslim faith it is a sin even to look at a temple, and this Dara had restored a railing in a temple! This fact is not creditable to the Muhammadans. Remove the railing.' By his order Abdun Nabi Khan (the faujdar of Mathura) removed it."--'Akhbarat', 9th year, sheet 7, (14 Oct., 1666).

20th Nov. 1665. "As it has come to His Majesty's knowledge that some inhabitants of the 'mahals' appertaining to the province of Gujrat have (again) built the temples which had been demolished by imperial order before his accession,. . .therefore His Majesty orders that. . .the formerly demolished and recently restored temples should be pulled down."--'Farman' given in 'Mirat', 273.

9th April, 1669. "The Emperor ordered the governors of all the provinces to demolish the schools and temples of the infidels and strongly put down their teaching and religious practices."--'Masir-i-Alamgiri', 81. (De Graaf, when at Hughli in 1670, heard of the order. Orme's 'Frag'., 250.)

May, 1669. "Salih Bahadur, mace-bearer, was sent to pull down the temple of Malarna."--M. A. 84.

2nd Sep. "News came to Court that according to the Emperor's command, his officers had demolished the temple of Vishwanath at Benares."--'Ibid'., 88.

(This was "the temple of Kirtti Visvesvara, at that time a modern shrine of Akbar's period."--Crooke's N.W.P., 112)

January, 1670. "In this month of Ramzan, the religious-minded Emperor ordered the demolition of the temple at Mathura known as the 'Dehra' of Keshav Rai. His officers accomplished it in a short time. A grand mosque was built on its site at a vast expenditure. The temple had been built by Bir Singh Dev Bundela, at a cost of 33 lakhs of Rupees. Praised be the God of the great faith of Islam that in the auspicious reign of this destroyer of infidelity and turbulence, such a marvellous and (seemingly) impossible feat was accomplished. On seeing this (instance of the) strength of the Emperor's faith and the grandeur of his devotion to God, the Rajahs felt suffocated and they stood in amazement like statues facing the walls. The idols, large and small, set with costly jewels, which had been set up in the temple, were brought to Agra and buried under the steps of the mosque of Jahanara, to be trodden upon continually."--'Ibid'., 95-96.

"He partially destroyed the Sitaramji temple at Soron; one of his officers slew the the priests, broke the image, and defiled the sanctuary at Devi Patan in Gonda."--Crooke's N.W.P., 112.

7th April, 1670. "News came from Malwa that Wazir Khan had sent Gada Beg, a slave, with 400 troopers, to destroy all temples around Ujjain. . .A Rawat of the place resisted and slew Gada Beg with 121 of his men."--'Akhbarat', 13th year, sheet 17.

"Order issued on all 'faujdars' of 'thanas', civil officers ('mutasaddis'), agents of jagirdars, 'kroris', and 'amlas' from Katak to Medinipur on the frontier of Orissa:--The imperial paymaster Asad Khan has sent a letter written by order of the Emperor, to say, that the Emperor learning from the news-letters of the province of Orissa that at the village of Tilkuti in Medinipur a temple has been (newly) built, has issued his august mandate for its destruction, and the destruction of all temples built anywhere in this province by the worthless infidels. Therefore, you are commanded with extreme urgency that immediately on the receipt of this letter you should destroy the above-mentioned temples. Every idol-house built during the last 10 or 12 years, whether with brick or clay, should be demolished without delay. Also, do not allow the crushed Hindus and despicable infidels to repair their old temples. Reports of the destruction of temples should be sent to the Court under the seal of the 'qazis' and attested by pious Shaikhs."--'Muraqat-i-Abul Hasan', (completed in 1670 A.D.) p. 202.

"In every 'pargana' officers have come from the 'thanas' with orders from the Presence for the destruction of idols."--A letter preserved in the Yasho-Madhav temple of Dhamrai in the Dacca district, dated 27 June, 1672, and printed in J. M. Ray's Bengali 'History of Dacca', i. 389.

"Darab Khan was sent with a strong force to punish the Rajputs of Khandela and demolish the great temple of that place." (M. A. 171.) "He attacked the place on 8th March, 1679, and pulled down the temples of Khandela and Sanula and all other temples in the neighbourhood." (M. A. 173.)

25 May 1679. "Khan-i-Jahan Bahadur returned from Jodhpur after demolishing its temples, and bringing with himself several cart-loads of idols. The Emperor ordered that the idols,--which were mostly of gold, silver, brass, copper or stone and adorned with jewels,--should be cast in the quadrangle of the Court and under the steps of the Jama Mosque for being trodden upon."--M. A. 175.

Jan. 1680. "The grand temple in front of the Maharana's mansion (at Udaipur)--one of the wonderful buildings of the age, which had cost the infidels much money--was destroyed and its images broken." (M. A. 168.) "On 24 Jan. the Emperor went to view the lake Udaisagar and ordered all the three temples on its banks to be pulled down" (p. 188.) "On 29 Jan. Hasan Ali Khan reported that 172 other temples in the environs of Udaipur had been demolished" (p 189.) "On 22nd Feb. the Emperor went to look at Chitor, and by his order the 63 temples of the place were destroyed" (p. 189.)

10 Aug. 1680. Abu Turab returned to Court and reported that he had pulled down 66 temples in Amber" (p. 194). 2 Aug. 1680. Temple of Someshwar in western Mewar ordered to be destroyed.--'Adab', 287 a and 290 a.

Sep. 1687. On the capture of Golkonda, the Emperor appointed Abdur Rahim Khan as Censor of the city of Haidarabad with orders to put down infidel practices and (heretical) innovations and destroy the temples and build mosques on their sites.--Khafi Khan, ii. 358-359.

'Circa' 1690. Instances of Aurangzib's temple destruction at Ellora, Trimbakeshwar, Narsinghpur (foiled by snakes, scorpions and other poisonous insects), Pandharpur, Jejuri (foiled by the deity!) and Yavat (Bhuleshwar) are given by K. N. Sane in 'Varshik Itibritta' for Shaka 1838, pp. 133-135.

1693. The Emperor ordered the destruction of the Hateshwar temple at Vadnagar, the special guardian of the Nagar Brahmans.--'Mirat', 346.

3rd April 1694. "The Emperor learnt from a secret news-writer of Delhi that in Jaisinghpura Bairagis used to worship idols, and that the Censor on hearing of it had gone there, arrested Sri Krishna Bairagi and taken him with 15 idols away to his house; then the Rajputs had assembled, flocked to the Censor's house, wounded three footmen of the Censor and tried to seize the Censor himself; so that the latter set the Bairagi free and sent the copper idols to the local subahdar."--Akhbarat, year 37, sheet 57.

Middle of 1698. "Hamid-ud-din Khan Bahadur who had been deputed to destroy the temple of Bijapur and build a mosque (there), returned to Court after carrying the order out and was praised by the Emperor."--M. A. 396.

"The demolition of a temple is possible at any time, as it cannot walk away from its place."--Aurangzib to Zulfiqar Khan and Mughal Khan in K. T., 39a.

"The houses of this country (Maharashtra) are exceedingly strong and built solely of stone and iron. The hatchet-men of the Government in the course of my marching do not get sufficient strength and power (i.e., time) to destroy and raze the temples of the infidels that meet the eye on the way. You should appoint an orthodox inspector ('darogha') who may afterwards destroy them at leisure and dig up their foundations,"--Aurangzib to Ruhullah Khan in 'Kalimat-i-Aurangzib', p. 34 of Rampur MS, and f.35a of I. O. L. MS. 3301.

1 Jan. 1705. "The Emperor, summoning Muhammad Khalil and Khidmat Rai, the 'darogha' of hatchet-men. . ., ordered them to demolish the temple of Pandharpur, and to take the butchers of the camp there and slaughter cows in the temple . . .It was done."--'Akhbarat', 49-7.

APPENDIX II

(By P. N. Oak)

THE TAJ MAHAL IS TEJO--MAHALAYA: A SHIVA TEMPLE

Probably there is none who has not been duped at least once in a life time. But can the whole world be duped? This may seem impossible. But in the matter of Indian history the world has been duped in many respects for hundreds of years and still continues to be duped.

The world famous Taj Mahal in Agra is a glaring instance. For all the time, money and energy that people the world over spend in visiting the Taj Mahal they are dished out a concoction. Contrary to what visitors are made to believe the Taj Mahal is not an Islamic mausoleum but an ancient Shiva temple known as Tejo Mahalaya which the 5th generation Mogul emperor Shahjahan commandeered from the then Maharaja of Jaipur. Therefore the Taj Mahal must be viewed as a temple-palace complex and not as a tomb. That makes a vast difference. You miss the details of its size, grandeur, majesty and beauty when you take it to be a mere tomb. When told that you are visiting a temple-palace complex you won't fail to notice its annexes, ruined defensive walls, hillocks, moats, cascades, fountains, majestic garden, hundreds of rooms, arcaded verandahs, terraces, multi-storied towers, secret sealed chambers, guest rooms, stables, the trident (trishul) pinnacle on the dome and the sacred, esoteric Hindu letter OM carved on the exterior of the wall of the sanctum sanctorum now occupied by the cenotaphs.

For detailed proof of this breath-taking discovery, you may read the well known book entitled "The Taj Mahal is a

Temple Palace". But let us place before you, for the time being an exhaustive summary of the massive evidence ranging over 103 points, namely:--

1. The term Taj Mahal itself never occurs in any Mogul court paper or chronicle even in Aurangzeb's time.

2. The attempt to explain it away as Taj-i-Mahal i.e. a crown among residences is, therefore, ridiculous.

3. Moreover, if the Taj is believed to be a burial place how can the term 'Mahal' i.e. 'mansion', apply to it?

4. The other popular Islamic explanation is that the term 'Taj Mahal' derives from 'Mumtaz Mahal'--the lady who is supposed to be buried in it. This explanation is itself full of absurdities as we shall presently see. It may be noted at the outset that the term 'Taj' which ends in a 'j', could not have been derived from Mumtaz ending in a 'z'.

5. Moreover, the lady's name was never Mumtaz Mahal but Arjumand Banu Begum alias Mumtaz-ul-Zamani, as mentioned in Shahjahan's official court chronicle, the Badshahnama.

6. Since the term Taj Mahal does not at all occur in Mogul records it is absurd to search for any Mogul explanation for it. Both its components namely 'Taj' and 'Mahal' are of Sanskritic origin. Mahal in Hindu parlance signifies a mansion i.e. a grand edifice. Taj is the popular corruption of the word 'Tej' meaning splendour. In no Muslim country from Afghanistan to Abyssinia, is any edifice described as Mahal.

7. The term Taj Mahal is a corrupt form of the Sanskrit term 'Tejo Mahalaya' signifying a Shiva temple. Agreshwar Mahadev i.e. the Lord God of Agra was consecrated in it.

8. The famous Hindu treatise on architecture, titled Viswakarma Vastushastra mentions the 'Tej Linga' amongst Shiva Lingas i.e. stone emblems of Lord Shiva, the Hindu

deity. Such a Teja Linga was consecrated in the Taj Mahal hence the term Taj Mahal alias Tejo Mahalaya.

9. Agra city, in which the Taj Mahal is located, is an ancient centre of Shiva worship. Its orthodox residents have through the ages continued the tradition of worshipping at five Shiva shrines before taking the last meal every night especially during the month of Shravan. During the last few centuries residents of Agra had to be content with worshipping at only four prominent Shiva temples viz. Balkeshwar, Prithvinath, Manakameshwar and Rajarajeshwar. They had lost track of the fifth Shiva deity which their forefathers worshipped. Apparently the fifth was Agreshwar Mahadev i.e. the Lord Great God of Agra consecrated in the Tejo-Mahalaya alias Taj Mahal.

10. The people who dominate the Agra region are Jats. Their name for Shiva is Tejaji. The Jat special issue of the Illustrated Weekly of India (June 28, 1971) mentions that the Jats have Teja Mandirs i.e. Teja temples. This is because Teja Linga is one among several names of Shiva Lingas mentioned in Hindu architectural texts. From this it is apparent that the Taj Mahal is Tejo Mahalaya, the Great Abode of Tej'.

11. A Sanskrit inscription too supports the above conclusion. Known as the Bateshwar inscription it is currently preserved in the Lucknow museum. It refers to the raising of a "Crystal white Shiva temple so alluring that Lord Shiva once enshrined in it decided never to return to Mount Kailas--his usual abode". This inscription was found within a radius of about 36 miles from the Taj Mahal. The inscription is dated 1155 A.D. From this it is clear that the Taj Mahal was built at least 500 years before Shahjahan.

12. Shahjahan's own court chronicle, the Badshahnama admits (on page 403, Vol. I) that a grand mansion of unique splendour, capped with a dome, (imaarat-e-alishan wa gumbaze) was taken from the Jaipur Maharaja Jaisingh for Mumtaz's burial.

13. The plaque put up by the archaeology department outside the Taj Mahal describes the edifice as a mausoleum built by Shahjahan for his wife Mumtaz Mahal, over 22 years from 1631 to 1653. That plaque is a specimen of historical bungling. Firstly, the plaque cites no authority for its claim. Secondly, the lady's name was Mumtaz-ul-Zamani and not Mumtaz Mahal. Thirdly, the period of 22 years is taken from some mumbo jumbo noting by an unreliable French visitor Tavernier, to the exclusion of all Muslim versions, which is an absurdity.

14. Prince Aurangzeb's letter to his father, emperor Shahjahan, belies the archaeological department's reliance on Tavernier. Aurangzeb's letter is recorded in at least two chronicles titled 'Aadaab-e-Alamgiri' and 'Yaadgaarnama'. In that Aurangzeb records in 1652 A.D. itself that the buildings in the fancied burial place of Mumtaz, were seven-storied and were so old that they were all leaking, while the dome had developed a crack on the northern side. Aurangzeb, therefore, ordered immediate repairs to the buildings at his own expense while recommending to the emperor that more elaborate repairs be carried out later. This is proof that during Shahjahan's reign itself the Taj complex was so old as to need immediate repairs.

15. The ex-Maharaja of Jaipur retains in his secret personal custody two orders from Shahjahan dated December 18, 1633 (bearing modern numbers K.D. 176 and 177) requisitioning the Taj building complex. That was so blatant a usurpation that the then ruler of Jaipur was ashamed to make the documents public.

16. The Rajasthan State Archives at Bikaner preserves three other firmans addressed by Shahjahan to Jaipur's ruler Jaisingh ordering the latter to supply marble from his Makrana quarries, and stone cutters. Jaisingh was apparently so enraged at the blatant seizure of the Taj Mahal that he refused to oblige Shahjahan by providing marble for grafting Koranic engravings and false tombs for further desecration of the Taj Mahal. Jaisingh looked upon Shahjahan's demand for marble and stone

cutters, as an insult added to injury.

17. The three firmans demanding marble were sent to Jaisingh within about two years of Mumtaz's death. Had Shahjahan really built the Taj Mahal over a period of 22 years the marble would have been needed only after 15 or 30 years and not immediately after Mumtaz's death.

18. Moreover, the three firmans mention neither the Taj Mahal, nor Mumtaz, nor the burial. The cost and the quantity of stone required also are not mentioned. This proves that an insignificant quantity of marble was needed just for some superficial tinkering and tampering with the Taj Mahal. Even otherwise Shahjahan could never hope to build a fabulous Taj Mahal by abject dependance for marble on a non-cooperative vassal like Jaisingh.

19. The Taj Mahal is scrawled over with 14 chapters of the Koran but nowhere is there even the slightest or remotest allusion in that Islamic overwriting to Shahjahan's authorship of the Taj. Had Shahjahan been the builder he would have said so in so many words before beginning to quote the Koran.

20. That Shahjahan far from building the marble Taj only disfigured it with black lettering is mentioned by the inscriber Amanat Khan Shirazi himself in an inscription on the building.

21. Well known western authorities on architecture like E. B. Havell, Mrs. Kenoyer and Sir W. W. Hunter have gone on record to say that the Taj Mahal is built in the Hindu temple style. Havell points out that the ground plan of the ancient Hindu Chandi Seva temple in Java is identical with that of the Taj.

22. A central dome with cupolas at its four corners is a universal feature of Hindu temples.

23. The four marble pillars at the plinth corners are of the Hindu style. They were used as lamp towers during the

night and as watch towers during the day. Such towers serve to demarcate the holy precincts. Hindu wedding altars and the altar set up for God Satyanarayan worship have pillars raised at the four corners.

24. The octagonal shape of the Taj Mahal has a special Hindu significance because Hindus alone have special names for the eight directions, and celestial guards assigned to them. The pinnacle points to the heaven while the foundation signifies the nether world. Hindu forts, cities, palaces, and temples generally have an octagonal layout or some octagonal features so that together with the pinnacle and the foundation they cover all the ten directions in which the king or god holds sway, according to Hindu belief.

25. The Taj Mahal has a trident pinnacle over the dome. A full scale figure of that trident pinnacle is inlaid in the red stone courtyard to the east of the Taj. The central shaft of the trident depicts a Kalash (sacred pot) holding two bent mango leaves and a coconut. This is a sacred Hindu motif. Identical pinnacles may be seen over Hindu and Buddhist temples in the Himalayan region. Tridents are also depicted against a red lotus background at the apex of the stately marble arched entrances on all four sides of the Taj Mahal. People fondly but mistakenly believed all these three centuries that the Taj pinnacle depicts an Islamic crescent and star or was a lightning conductor installed by the British rulers of India. Contrarily the pinnacle is a marvel of Hindu metallurgy since the pinnacle made of a non-rusting alloy, is also perhaps a lightning deflector. That the replica of the pinnacle is drawn in the eastern courtyard is significant because the east is of special importance to the Hindus, as the direction in which the sun rises. The pinnacle on the dome has the word Allah carved on it after capture. The pinnacle figure on the ground does not have the word Allah.

26. The two buildings which face the marble Taj from the east and west are identical in design, size and shape and yet the eastern building is explained away by Islamic

tradition, as a community hall while the western building is claimed to be a mosque. How could buildings meant for radically different purposes be identical? This proves that the western building was put to use as a mosque after seizure of the Taj property by Shahjahan. Curiously enough the building being explained away as a mosque has no minaret.

27. A few yards away on the same flank is the Nakkar Khana alias drum house which is an intolerable incongruity for Islam. The proximity of the drum house indicates that the western annex was not originally a mosque. Contrarily a drum house is a necessity in a Hindu temple or palace because Hindu chores morning and evening begin to the sweet strains of music.

28. The embossed patterns on the marble exterior of the cenotaph chamber wall are foliage of the conch shell design and the Hindu letter 'OM'. The octagonally laid marble lattices inside the cenotaph chamber depict pink lotuses on their top railing. The lotus, the OM and the conch shell are sacred motifs associated with Hindu deities and temples.

29. The spot occupied by Mumtaz's cenotaph was formerly occupied by the Hindu Teja Linga--a lithic representation of Lord Shiva. That emblem may still lie buried in the cenotaph for all we know. Around it are three perambulatory passages. Perambulation could be done around the marble lattice or through the spacious marble chambers surrounding the cenotaph chamber, and in the open over the marble platform. It is also customary for Hindus to have apertures along the perambulatory passage, overlooking the deity. Such apertures exist in the perambulatories in the Taj Mahal.

30. The sanctum sanctorum in the Taj Mahal had silver doors and gold railings as Hindu temples still have. It also had nets of pearl, and gems stuffed in the marble lattices. It was the lure of this wealth which made Shahjahan commandeer the Taj Mahal from a helpless vassal Jaisingh, the then ruler of Jaipur.

31. Peter Mundy an Englishman who left India within a year or two of Mumtaz's death notes having seen a gem-studded gold railing around Mumtaz's tomb. Had the Taj Mahal been under construction for 22 years a costly gold railing would not have been noticed by Peter Mundy within a couple of years of Mumtaz's death. Such costly fixtures are installed in a building only after the building is ready for use. This indicates that Mumtaz's cenotaph was grafted in the centre of the gold railings. Subsequently the gold railings, silver doors, nets of pearls, gem-fillings etc. were all carted away to Shahjahan's treasury. The seizure of the Taj Mahal thus constituted an act of high-handed Mogul robbery which occasioned a big tussle between Shahjahan and Jaisingh.

32. In the marble flooring around Mumtaz's cenotaph may be seen tiny mosaic patches. Those patches indicate the spots where the supports for the gold railings were embedded in the floor. They indicate a rectangular fencing.

33. Above Mumtaz's cenotaph, hangs a chain by which now hangs a lamp. Before capture by Shahjahan the chain used to hold a water pitcher from which water used to drip on the Shiva Linga.

34. It is this earlier drip-drop Hindu tradition in the Taj Mahal which gave rise to the Islamic myth of Shahjahan's love tear dropping on Mumtaz's tomb on a full moon day on winter eve.

35. There are many absurdities in the Shahjahan tear legend. Firstly, Shahjahan was no saint capable of post-mortem miracles. Secondly, why should only one lone tear drop on the cenotaph in 365 days from a proverbially disconsolate Shahjahan? Even that tear could be shed by Shahjahan's ghost entering the chamber through the public entrance to weep his heart out on Mumtaz's tombstone itself. Why should Shahjahan's ghost perform a precarious circus feat of clambering up a slippery marble dome which even an agile monkey won't dare

attempt, and shed one tear once a year from a height over 200 feet?

The tear is said to drop in the form of dew or rain water, at the stroke of the midnight hour through a tiny needle hole aperture made by an irate mason's random hammer stroke. This gives rise to many more absurdities viz. is the liquid the secretion of Shahjahan's ghost or dew or rain? Furthermore there is no aperture in the dome as is claimed or assumed. Had there been any such, rain water would have leaked in too and made the interior wet. Moreover, the Taj Mahal has a double dome. The concave dome one sees from inside, ends like a huge inverted pan on the terrace. The dome one sees from the outside rests like a top hat on the inner dome. Inside it is a huge chamber about 83 feet high with the convex top of the inner dome providing a curious domed floor. Because of this double dome arrangement no liquid, including Shahjahan's tear can even drop inside the Taj. Even if the upper, dome has a chance aperture the drop, if any, will be arrested by the inner dome. This is a typical instance of how gullible multitudes place quick and easy faith in the most absurd concoctions.

36. Even the hammer-story is a fabrication. Firstly, nobody seems to ask why should any mason bear any grudge towards Shahjahan when the latter is said to have spent liberally and lavishly in commissioning the mausoleum? Secondly, even if a mason bore any grudge he would not be permitted access to the emperor to exchange hot words with. Even if there were any argument between the two it would not be between a Shahjahan standing in the garden and the petulant mason on the slippery perch like an irate monkey on top of the dome at a perpendicular height of 243 feet or so. What is more, an angry mason's most powerful hammer stroke would not make even the slightest dent in the dome because the dome has a 13 feet thick wall covered with hard marble.

The hammer stroke and tear drop stories are a fraudulent Islamic fabrication based on two facts. One of those we have already noted namely that in the Hindu tradition water did drip in droplets from a pitcher hung over the Shiva Linga.

The second fact is that Shahjahan was so stingy by nature that he did not want to spend even a cent from his own treasury in transforming a captured Taj Mahal into an Islamic mausoleum. His troops used to round up workers from Agra city and the neighbourhood at sword point or at the crack of a whip. Such forced labour was employed for years in pulling out Hindu idols, grafting Koranic engravings, and sealing, five of the seven stories of the Taj Mahal. Being compelled to work for years without wages, the workmen rebelled. A haughty Shahjahan punished them by amputating their hands.

37. But the above gruesome detail has been given a romantic twist by fabricators of the Shahjahan legend. They want people to believe that Shahjahan maimed the workers because they should not build a rival Taj for someone else. This facile, disingenious version is based on many imponderable details. Firstly, for anybody to conceive a rival Taj he should have had as comely and infatuating a wife as Mumtaz is believed to have been. Secondly, she should have died after the Taj Mahal was supposed to have been completed by Shahjahan. Thirdly, that fancied prospective rival should be swayed by tearing envy and jealousy. Fourthly, he must be as affluent as a Mogul emperor and be an equally irresponsible spendthrift itching to squander his millions on a fabulous mausoleum. Even if all this fantastic nonsense is conjured up as a reality, an angry Shahjahan could still nip the competitive impudence of a subject of his by a simple imperial fiat prohibiting the buiding of a rival Taj.

A further absurdity is that while on the one hand it is contended that Shahjahan was so soft hearted as to weep disconsolately over the death of his wife, it is also contended in the same breath that he turned fiercely treacherous as soon as the wonder mausoleum was complete and ordered the maimimg of the master workmen. Would a sovereign be gratified and reward the master craftsmen who execute a work of art or would he punish them with maiming for all their skill and devotion? Such rascality and treachery not attributed even to a snake is unwittingly attributed to Shahjahan by his absentminded admirers.

38. As one climbs down the stairs to the basement chamber in the Taj, believed to house the real grave of Mumtaz, one may take a close look at the walls on either side of the first landing. The walls are finished with marble slabs of dissimilar sizes. That indicates that ramps or stairs branching off at the first landing, to go down to the other chambers in the basement have been sealed off by Shahjahan haphazardly with dissimilar slabs which came handy.

39. Apart from these stairs there are many others which have been sealed by Shahjahan. As one climbs up from the red stone courtyard to the marble plinth one may notice a square marble slab in front. Stamping one's feet on it one gets a hollow sound. Thumping on the surrounding slabs does not produce a hollow sound. Apparently the square slab hides a man-size entrance to a staircase leading to hidden chambers in the marble basement. Another steep staircase sealed by Shahjahan was discovered when a stone slab on the terrace beyond the so-called mosque and octagonal well, was removed for investigation when a chance thumping produced a hollow sound there. This indicates the extent of Shahjahan's tampering with the Taj and that there is much more to see and discover in the Taj, than meets the eye.

40. The Taj Mahal having originated as a temple palace it has several dry, scavenging type toilets which lie unknown to the lay visitor, locked and barred. Had it been an Islamic mausoleum it should not have had toilets.

41. Between the so-called mosque and the drum house is a multi-storied octagonal well with a flight of stairs reaching down to the water level. This is the traditional treasury well in Hindu temple palaces. Treasure chests used to be kept in the lower apartments while treasury personnel had their offices in the upper chambers. The circular stairs made it difficult for intruders to reach down to the treasure or to escape with it undetected or unpursued. In case the premises had to be surrendered to a besieging enemy the treasure could be pushed into the well to remain hidden from the conqueror and remain

safe for salvaging if the place was reconquered. Such an elaborate multi-storied well is superfluous for a mere mausoleum.

42. Tavernier, a French merchant who happened to visit India during Shahjahan's reign has noted in his memoirs that Shahjahan "purposely" buried Mumtaz at the "the Taj-i-Macan", (i.e. the Taj Mahal) so that the world may admire the burial spot because even foreigners used to flock to see the Taj Mahal in Tavernier's time as they do now. Those who are misled to believe that the Taj Mahal finds no mention before Mumtaz's death, may note Tavernier's reference.

43. Had Shahjahan really built the Taj Mahal as a wonder mausoleum, history would have recorded a specific date on which she was ceremoniously buried in the Taj Mahal. No such date is ever mentioned. This important missing detail decisively exposes the falsity of the Shahjahan legend.

44. Even the year of Mumtaz's death is unknown. It is variously speculated to be 1629, 1630, 1631 or 1632. Had she deserved a fabulous burial, as is claimed, the date of her death would not have been a matter of speculation. In a harem teeming with 5000 women it was difficult to keep track of dates of death. Apparently the date of Mumtaz's death was so insignificant an event as not to merit any special notice. Who would then build a Taj Mahal for her burial?

45. Stories of Shahjahan's exclusive infatuation for Mumtaz are concoctions. They have no basis in history nor has any book ever been written on their fancied love affair. Those stories have been invented as an after-thought to make Shahjahan's authorship of the Taj, look plausible.

46. The cost of the Taj Mahal is nowhere recorded in Shahjahan's court papers because Shahjahan never built the Taj Mahal. That is why wild estimates of the cost by gullible writers have ranged from four million to 91.7 million rupees.

47. Likewise the period of construction has been guessed to be anywhere between 10 and 22 years. There would not have been any scope for such guesswork had the building construction been on record in the court papers.

48. The designer of the Taj Mahal is also variously mentioned as Essa Effendy, a Persian or Turk or Ahmed Mehendis or a Frenchman, Austin de Bordeaux or Geronimo Veroneo an Italian or Shahjahan himself.

49. Twenty thousand labourers are supposed to have worked for 22 years during Shahjahan's reign in building the Taj Mahal. Had this been true, there should have been available in Shahjahan's court papers heaps of labour muster rolls, daily expenditure sheets, bills and receipts for material ordered, and commissioning orders. There is not even a scrap of paper of the kind.

50. It is, therefore, court flatterers, fiction writers and senile poets who are responsible for hustling the world into believing in Shahjahan's mythical authorship of the Taj Mahal.

51. Descriptions of the garden around the Taj of Shahjahan's time mention Ketaki, Jai, Ji, Champa, Maulashree, Harshringar and Bel. All these are plants whose flowers or leaves are used in the worship of Hindu deities. Bel leaves are used exclusively in Shiva worship. A graveyard is planted only with shady trees because the idea of using fruit or flower from plants in a cemetery is abhorrent to human conscience. The presence of Bel and other flower plants in the Taj garden is proof of its having been a Shiva temple before seizure by Shahjahan.

52. Hindu temples are often built on river banks and sea beaches. The Taj Mahal is one such built on the bank of the Yamuna river--an ideal location for a Shiva temple.

53. Prophet Mohammad has ordained that the burial spot of a Muslim should be inconspicuous and must not be marked by even a single tombstone. In flagrant violation of this the Taj Mahal has one grave in the basement and

another in the first floor chamber both ascribed to Mumtaz. Those two cenotaphs were in fact erected by Shahjahan to bury the two tier Shiva Lingas that were consecrated in the Taj Mahal. It is customary for Hindus to install two Shiva Lingas one over the other in two stories as may be seen in the Mahankaleshwar temple in Ujjain and the Somnath temple raised by Ahilyabai in Somnath Pattan.

54. The Taj Mahal has identical entrance arches on all four sides. This is a typical Hindu building style known as Chaturmukhi i.e. four-faced.

55. The Taj Mahal has a reverberating dome. Such a dome is an absurdity for a tomb which must ensure peace and silence. Contrarily reverberating domes are a necessity in Hindu temples because they create an ecstatic din multiplying and magnifying the sound of bells, drums and pipes accompanying the worship of Hindu deities.

56. The Taj Mahal dome bears a lotus cap. Original Islamic domes have a bald top as is exemplified by the Pakistan Embassy domes in Chanakyapuri, New Delhi and the domes in Pakistan's newly built capital Islamabad.

57. The Taj Mahal entrance faces south. Had the Taj been an Islamic building it should have faced the west.

58. A widespread misunderstanding has resulted in mistaking the building for the grave. Invading Islam raised graves in captured buildings in every country it overran. Therefore, hereafter people must learn not to confound the building with the grave mounds which are grafts in conquered buildings. This is true of the Taj Mahal too.

59. The Taj Mahal is a seven-storied building. Prince Aurangzeb also mentions this in his letter to Shahjahan. The marble edifice comprises four stories including the lone, tall circular hall inside the dome on top, and the lone chamber in the basement. In between are two floors each containing 12 to 15 palatial rooms.

Below the marble plinth reaching down to the river at the rear are two more stories in red stone. They may be seen from the river bank. The seventh story must be below the ground (river) level since every ancient Hindu buiding had a subterranian story.

60.   Immediately below the marble plinth on the river flank are 22 rooms in red stone with their ventilators all walled up by Shahjahan.

Those rooms made uninhabitably dark by Shahjahan are kept locked by the archaeology department. The lay visitor is kept in the dark about them. Those 22 rooms still bear ancient Hindu paint on their walls and ceilings. On their inner side is a nearly 300 ft. long corridor. There are two door frames one at either end of the corridor. but those doorways are intriguingly sealed with crumbling brick and lime.

61.   Apparently those doorways originally sealed by Shah-jahan have been since unsealed and again walled up several times. In 1934 a resident of Delhi took a peep inside from an opening in the upper part of the doorway. To his dismay he saw a huge hall inside. It contained many statues huddled around a central beheaded image of Lord Shiva. It could be that in there are Sanskrit inscriptions too. All the seven stories of the Taj Mahal need to be unsealed and scoured to ascertain what evidence they may be hiding in the form of Hindu images, Sanskrit inscriptions, scriptures, coins and uten-sils.

62.   Apart from Hindu images hidden in the sealed stories it is learnt that Hindu images are also buried in the massive walls of the Taj Mahal. Between 1959 and 1962 when Mr. S. R. Rao was the archeological superinten-dent in Agra he happened to notice a long, deep and wide crack in a wall of the central octagonal chamber of the Taj. When a part of the wall was dismantled to study the crack out popped two or three marble images.   The matter was hushed up and the images were reburied where they had been embedded at Shahjahan's behest. Confirmation of this has been obtained from several

sources. It was only when I began my investigation into the antecedents of the Taj that I came across the above information which had remained a forgotten secret.

What better proof is needed of the temple origin off the Taj Mahal? Its walls and sealed chambers still hide the Hindu idols that were consecrated in it before Shahjahan's seizure of the Taj Mahal.

63. Apparently the Taj Mahal as a temple palace seems to have had a chequered history. The Taj was perhaps desecrated and looted by every Muslim invader from Mohammad Ghazni onwards but passing into Hindu hands off and on the sanctity of the Taj Mahal as a Shiva temple continued to be revived after every Muslim onslaught. Shahjahan was the last Muslim to desecrate the Taj Mahal alias Tejo Mahalaya.

64. Vincent Smith records in his book titled "Akbar the Great Mogul" that "Babur's turbulent life came to an end in his garden palace in Agra" in 1630. That palace was none other than the Taj Mahal.

65. Babur's daughter Gulbadan Begum in her chronicle titled Humayun Nama refers to the Taj Mahal as the Mystic House.

66. Babur himself refers to the Taj Mahal in his memoirs as a palace captured from Ibrahim Lodi containing a central octagonal chamber and having pillars on the four sides. All these historical references allude to the Taj Mahal 100 years before Shahjahan.

67. The Taj Mahal precincts extend to several hundred yards in all directions. Across the river are ruins of the annexes of the Taj, the bathing ghats and a jetty for the ferry boat. In the Victoria gardens outside covered with creepers is a long spur of the ancient outer wall ending in an octagonal red stone tower. Such extensive grounds all magnificently done up are a superfluity for a grave.

68. Had the Taj been built specially to bury Mumtaz, in it should not have been cluttered with other graves. But the Taj premises contain several other graves at least in its eastern and southern pavilions.

69. In the southern flank on either side of the Tajgan gate are buried in identical pavilions a queen Sarhandi Begum and a maid Satunnisa Khanum. Such parity burial can be justified only if the queen has been demoted or the maid promoted. But since Shahjahan had commandeered (not built) the Taj Mahal he reduced it indiscriminately to a general Muslim cemetery as was the habit of all his Islamic predecessors, and buried a queen in one vacant pavilion and a maid in another identical pavilion.

70. Shahjahan was married to several other women before and after Mumtaz. She, therefore deserved no special consideration in having a wonder mausoleum built for her.

71. Mumtaz was also a commoner by birth and so she did not qualify for a fairyland burial.

72. Mumtaz died in Burhanpur which is about six hundred miles from Agra. Her grave there is intact. Therefore, the cenotaphs raised in two stories of the Taj, in her name seem to be fakes hiding the Hindu Shiva emblems.

73. Shahjahan seems to have simulated Mumtaz's burial in Agra to find a pretext to surround the temple palace with his fierce and fanatic Islamic troops and remove all its costly fixtures to his treasury. This finds confirmation in the vague noting in the official chronicle, the Badshahnama which says that Mumtaz's (exhumed) body was brought to Agra from Burhanpur and buried "next year". An official chronicle wouldn't use a nebulous term unless it is to hide something.

74. A pertinent consideration is that a Shahjahan who did not build any palaces for Mumtaz while she was alive and kicking would not build a fabulous mausoleum for a corpse which was no longer kicking or clicking.

75. Another factor is that Mumtaz died within two to three years of Shahjahan becoming emperor. Could he amass so much superfluous wealth in that short span as to squander it on a wonder mausoleum?

76. While Shahjahan's special attachment to Mumtaz is nowhere recorded in history his amorous affairs with many other ladies from maids to mannequins including his own daughter Jahanara find special mention in accounts of Shahjahan's reign. Would such a Shahjahan shower his hard-earned wealth on Mumtaz's corpse?

77. Shahjahan was a stingy, usurious monarch. He came to the throne murdering all his rivals. He was not, therefore, the doting spendthrift that he is made out to be.

78. A Shahjahan disconsolate on Mumtaz's death is suddenly credited with a resolve to build the Taj. This is a psychological incongruity. Grief is a disabling, incapacitating emotion.

79. An infatuated Shahjahan is supposed to have raised the Taj over a dead Mumtaz, but carnal, physical, sexual love is again an incapacitating emotion. A womanizer is ipso facto incapable of any constructive activity. When carnal love becomes uncontrollable the person either murders somebody or commits suicide. He cannot raise a Taj Mahal. A building like the Taj Mahal invariably originates in an enobling emotion like devotion to god, to one's mother and mother country or power and glory.

80. Early in the year 1973 chance digging in the garden infront of the Taj revealed another set of fountains about six feet below the present fountains. This proved two things. Firstly, that the subterranean fountains were there before Shahjahan laid the surface fountains. And secondly that since those fountains are aligned to the Taj that edifice too is of pre-Shahjahan origin. Apparently the garden and its fountains had sunk from annual monsoon flooding and lack of maintenance for centuries during Islamic rule.

81. The stately rooms on the upper floor of the Taj Mahal have been stripped of their marble mosaic by Shahjahan to obtain matching marble for raising fake tomb stones inside the Taj premises at several places. Contrasting with the rich, marble finished ground floor rooms the stripping of the marble mosaic covering the lower half of the walls and flooring of the upper story chambers have given those rooms a naked, robbed, look. Since no visitors are allowed entry to the upper story this despoilation by Shahjahan has remained a well-guarded secret. There is no reason why Shahjahan's loot of the upper floor marble should continue to be hidden from the public even after two hundred years of termination of Mogul rule.

82. Bernier, a French traveler has recorded that no non-Muslim was allowed entry into the secret nether chambers of the Taj because there were some dazzling costly fixtures there. Had those been installed by Shahjahan they should have been shown to the public as a matter of pride. But since it was commandeered Hindu wealth Shahjahan dared not show it to others lest it lead to attempts at recapture.

83. The approach to the Taj Mahal is dotted with hillocks raised with earth dug out from foundation trenches. The hillocks served as outer defences of the Taj building complex. Raising such hillocks from foundation earth, is a common Hindu device of hoary origin. Nearby Bharatpur provides a graphic parallel.

     Peter Mundy has recorded that Shahjahan employed thousands of labourers to level some of those hillocks. This is graphic proof of the Taj Mahal existing before Shahjahan.

84. Tavernier, the French traveller has noted that Shahjahan couldn't obtain timber for raising a scaffolding (to inscribe the Koran at various heights). Shahjahan had, therefore, to raise a scaffolding of brick. As a result the "cost of the scaffolding was more than that of the entire

work" says Tavernier. This is clear proof that Shahjahan did not build the Taj but only inscribed the Koran.

85. The spiked gates at the various archways in the Taj premises, and the moat still seen on the eastern flank are defence devices not needed for a mausoleum.

86. According to the Encyclopaedia Britannica the Taj building complex consists of guest rooms, guard rooms and stables. These are irrelevant for a mausoleum.

87. At the backside river bank is a Hindu crematorium, a Shiva temple and bathing ghats of ancient origin. Had Shahjahan built the Taj Mahal, he would have destroyed those Hindu features.

88. The story that Shahjahan wanted to build a black marble Taj across the river, is another motivated myth. The ruins dotting the other side of the river are those of Hindu structures demolished during Muslim invasions and not the plinth of another Taj Mahal. A Shahjahan who did not build the white marble Taj would hardly ever think of building a black marble Taj. He was so miserly that he forced labourers to work gratis even in the superficial tampering necessary to make a Hindu temple serve as a Muslim tomb.

89. The marble that Shahjahan used for grafting Koranic lettering in the Taj is of a pale white shade while the rest of the Taj Mahal is built with marble of a rich yellow tint. That disparity is proof of the Koranic extracts being a superimposition.

90. Though imaginative attempts have been made by some historians to foist some fictitious name on history as the designer of the Taj Mahal others more imaginative have credited Shahjahan himself with superb architectural proficiency and artistic talent which could easily conceive and even plan the Taj even in acute bereavement. Such people betray gross ignorance of history inasmuch as Shahjahan was a cruel tyrant, a great womanizer and a drug and drink addict.

91. Fanciful accounts about Shahjahan commissioning the Taj are all confused. Some assert that Shahjahan ordered building drawings from all over the world and chose one from among them. Others assert that a man at hand was ordered to design a mausoleum and his design was approved. Had any of those versions been true Shahjahan's court papers should have had thousands of drawings concerning the Taj but there is not even one drawing. This is yet another clinching proof that Shahjahan did not commission the Taj.

92. The Taj Mahal is surrounded by huge ruined mansions which indicate that great battles have been waged around the Taj several times.

93. At the southeast corner of the Taj garden is an ancient royal cattle house. Cows attached to the Tejo Mahalaya temple used to be reared there. A cowshed is an incongruity in an Islamic tomb.

94. On the western flank of the Taj are several stately red stone annexes. These are superfluous for a mausoleum.

95. The entire Taj complex comprises 400 to 500 rooms. Residential accommodation on such a stupendous scale is unthinkable in a mausoleum.

96. The neighbouring Tajganj township's massive protective wall also encloses the Taj Mahal temple palace complex. This is clear indication that the Tejo-Mahalaya temple palace was part and parcel of the township. A street of that township leads straight into the Taj Mahal. The Tajganj gate is aligned in a perfect straight line to the octagonal red stone garden gate and the stately entrance arch of the marble Taj Mahal. The Tajganj gate besides being central to the Taj temple complex, is also put on a pedestal. The western gate by which visitors enter the Taj complex these days is a comparatively minor gateway. It has become the entry gate for most visitors today because the railway station and the bus station are on that side.

97. The Taj Mahal has pleasure pavilions which a tomb would never have.

98. A tiny mirror glass in a gallery of the Red Fort in Agra reflects the Taj Mahal. Shahjahan is said to have spent the last eight years of his life as a prisoner in that gallery peering at the reflected Taj Mahal and sighing in the name of Mumtaz. This myth is a blend of many falsehoods. Firstly, old Shahjahan was held prisoner by his son Aurangzeb in a basement story in the fort and not in an open, fashionable upper story. Secondly, that glass piece was fixed in the 1930's by Insha Allah Khan, a peon of the archeology department, just to illustrate to the visitors how in ancient times the entire apartment used to scintillate with tiny mirror pieces reflecting the Tejo Mahalaya temple a thousand fold. Thirdly, an old decrepit Shahjahan with pain in his joints and cataract in his eyes, would not spend the day craning his neck at an awkward angle to peer into a tiny glass piece with bedimmed eyesight when he could as well turn his face round and have a full, direct view of the Taj Mahal itself. But the general public is so gullible as to gulp all such absurd prattle of wily, unscrupulous guides.

99. That the Taj Mahal dome has hundreds of iron rings sticking out of its exterior is a feature rarely noticed. These are made to hold Hindu earthen oil lamps for temple illumination.

100. Those putting implicit faith in Shahjahan's authorship of the Taj have been imagining Shahjahan-Mumtaz to be a soft-hearted romantic pair like Romeo and Juliet. But contemporary accounts speak of Shahjahan as a hard hearted ruler who was constantly egged on to acts of tyranny and cruelty, by Mumtaz.

101. School and college history books carry the myth that Shahjahan's reign was a golden period in which there was peace and plenty and that Shahjahan commissioned many buildings and patronized literature. This is a pure fabrication. Shahjahan did not commission even a single building as we have illustrated by a detailed analysis of the

Taj Mahal legend. Shahjahan had to engage in 48 military campaigns during a reign of nearly 30 years which proves that his was not an era of peace and plenty.

102. The interior of the dome, rising over Mumtaz's cenotaph, has a representation of the Sun drawn in gold. Hindu warriors trace their origin to the Sun. For an Islamic mausoleum the Sun is redundant.

103. The Muslim caretakers of the tombs in the Taj Mahal used to possess a document which they styled as "Tarikh -i-Taj Mahal." Historian H. G. Keene has branded it as "a document of doubtful authenticity". Keene was uncannily right since we have seen that Shahjahan not being the creator of the Taj Mahal any document which credits Shahjahan with the Taj Mahal, must be an outright forgery. Even that forged document is reported to have been since smuggled out to Pakistan.

The Taj Mahal is only a typical illustration of how all historic buildings and townships from Kashmir to Cape Comorin though of hoary Hindu origin have been ascribed to this or that Muslim ruler or courtier.

It is hoped that people the world over who study Indian history will awaken to this new finding and revise their erstwhile beliefs.

Those interested in an in-depth study of the above and many other revolutionary rebuttals may read this author's other research books.

(By Colin Maine)

THE DEAD HAND OF ISLAM

There has been a resurgence of Islam recently. This has plunged the countries where this has happened into the dark ages. They have been set back a thousand years.

In THE SYDNEY MORNING HERALD dated 13.2.79 it was reported that Pakistan is going to bring back stoning. Moslems caught drinking alcohol will be given 80 lashes, and thieves will have either their foot or hand cut off.

In Iran men are sent to the firing squads on charges of "warring against God and his emissaries". Courts have frozen pending divorces by women.

"Three girls' secondary schools were closed after being raided by Khomeini's supporters, and unveiled women were being attacked in the streets. . .Women who were protesting about Khomeini's speech telling women in the government to wear clothes covering hair, neck, arms and feet, were threatened with shouts of 'get dressed or get beaten'."

Also in Iran, Moslem demonstrators shouting "purification by fire", set alight the red light district in Tehran. Prostitutes were attacked, brothels, bars and nightclubs looted.

An Abadan cinema was set alight and 377 people were burnt alive. Those who set fire to it closed the exit doors from the outside, and systematically set it ablaze at its four corners. NEWSWEEK, September 4, 1978 reported that there had been 30 cinema fires in Iran in the previous month.

It was reported on February 6, 1978 that the 23-year-old Princess Misha was executed in Jiddah either for marrying a commoner or adultery.

In Malaysia Moslem fanatics have been invading Hindu temples and smashing their images and gods. This could start

147

a religious war. There are some Moslems who are demanding that the Islamic punishment of stoning and whipping be imposed.

On the Australian Broadcasting Commission radio news on May 9, 1979 it was reported that in Iran militant Moslems announced that they intended to convert the world to Islam, and that their first task was to "root out deviations."

These events are not as Moslems apologists assert, aberrations but an inevitable outcome of the basic teachings of Islam. All can be justified either by the KORAN or by the HADITHS--the traditions concerning the acts and sayings of Mohammed. Both are considered a guide as to how life should be ordered in an Islamic society.

The KORAN was written down 20 years after Mohammed's death, and the first HADITH 220 years after his death. Many HADITHS were invented in the intervening years to support a particular course of action.

According to both HADITH and KORAN, Islam must be the world's most oppressive religion. It is undemocratic; it is puritanical; it is barbarously punitive; it oppresses women; its laws are cruel to animals; it is intolerant towards other religions; it is anti-intellectual; it places restrictions upon art.

CRUEL PUNISHMENTS

CRUCIFIXION. This is permitted by the KORAN for "Making war against Allah and his messengers".

FLOGGING. 100 lashes is given for adultery or fornication. 80 lashes is given for bearing false witness. (Here this is only mentioned in reference to charges against chaste women).

Flogging is also given for drinking alcohol.   No punishment is prescribed in the KORAN for this. It merely states that it is a sin and an abomination. In practice in many Moslem countries, 80 lashes is the penalty for merely drinking a glass of wine.

Yet there is no mention whatever in the KORAN about drugs, and in countries like Iran where alcohol is strictly forbidden, there are estimated to be 2 million drug addicts; heroin and hashish are openly sold in the streets, and "addicts huddle by an open drain with rags over their heads inhaling amid a stench of stale urine."

MUTILATION. "As to the thief, male or female, cut off his or her hands." So not just one hand is to be cut off but both of them.

WOMEN TO BE IMMURED. "If any of your women are guilty of lewdness, take the evidence of four reliable witnesses from amongst you against them; and if they testify, confine them to their houses until Death do claim them, or Allah ordain for them some other way." So for some vague sexual trifle women can be locked up for their entire life.

PENALTY FOR MURDER. The KORAN seems to regard sexual misdemeanours as being more reprehensible than murder. For killing another human being, one has only to make a compensation to the relatives of the person killed. These are the only references I could find in the KORAN to punishment, so for most crimes we have to rely on the HADITH.

STONING. Though there is no mention in the KORAN about stoning for adultery, Mohammed did use the punishment according to a HADITH. One account says that a man who had become a Moslem confessed to fornication. Mohammed ordered him to be stoned at the Musalla (Mosque outside Medina). When the stones struck him he ran away, but he was caught and stoned until he was dead. Then Mohammed spoke well of him and prayed over him.

Another HADITH relates that a Jew and Jewess were brought before Mohammed for fornication. Omar relates: "They were stoned on the level ground and I saw the man leaning over the woman to shield her from the stones."

I find this story rather far fetched, as it relates that the Jew was brought a BIBLE, and was told to read from it. He is supposed to have tried to cover the words about stoning with his hand. He would have been extremely stupid to have tried to do this in full view of a group of Moslems, as this would only draw attention to the words.

Women will be happy to know that it is considered laudable to spare their modesty should they be stoned. A hole dug, and she is buried up to her waist before she is killed by having rocks thrown at her.

The DICTIONARY OF ISLAM says that stoning "has become almost obsolete in modern times." So this religion is becoming more repressive, not less. The victims will be happy to know that they will get the full funeral rites.

THE OPPRESSION OF WOMEN

Islam is very harsh on women, particularly in sexual matters. The KORAN says: "Your wives are as tilth unto you. So approach your tilth when or how ye will." The word 'tilth' comes from till--to work by plowing, sowing, and raising crops from.

So a man can have sex with one of his wives at any time, and in any way that he wants. The woman does not have similar rights. As punishment, the KORAN says that if women are disloyal their husbands should refuse to sleep with them. Sexuality in women seems to be considered undesirable. The KORAN ways that slaves girls should be "chaste, not lustful." In the Moslem heaven men will be given dark-eyed virgins who are perpetually young. There is no mention of women being provided with virile young men, so they had better take their knitting with them as there will be little else to do. The only pleasures described in the KORAN are sitting on thrones, walking through gardens eating fruits, and drinking heavily wine (which does not even intoxicate).

As Ramon Lull said of it: What will their paradise be but a tavern of unwearied gorging, and a brothel of perpetual turpitude?"

ISLAM HYPOCRITICAL ON SEX

The Moslem religion is completely hypocritical on sexual matters and it is all in favor of the men. The mere performance of ceremony permits a man to have sex with any of his four wives in any manner and at any time.

Also the KORAN permits men to use women captured in war for their sexual amusement. They can also be bought. Mohammed himself received two slave girls as a present from the governor of Egypt. One he gave to a man called Hassan, and the other he kept for himself, and she subsequently had a son by him. The KORAN allows a Moslem to have as many concubines as he wants.

The SOCIAL LAWS OF THE KORAN says: ". . .he is permitted to cohabit with his female slave. In this case nothing is said as to number; they are allowed to him without any restriction whatever."

Yet Islam punishes women more severely than men for sexual offenses. In a Moslem country this year a man and a woman were flogged for adultery. The man got 25 lashes and the woman 100 lashes.

On June 19, 1979 it was reported in THE AUSTRALIAN that an Iranian woman was executed for having illicit sexual relations. The man involved got a lighter sentence. The report said that the woman was put to death by her mother, father and a brother.

Though he placed such severe restrictions on women, Mohammed himself had as much sex as he wanted. His wife Ayesha who he married when she was 10, and he was 53 said of Mohammed: "He loved three things, women, perfume and food, and of the first two he had his heart's desire.

Mohammed had 11 wives, as well as concubines, even though he restricted his followers to four wives. A 'special revelation' from Allah permitted him to have as many wives as he liked. Oddly enough his revelations always seemed to tell him the sort of things that he wanted to know.

We have already seen that women can be punished for lewdness with life imprisonment. Yet the following verse of the KORAN says: "If two men among you are guilty of lewdness, punish them both. If they repent and amend let them both alone."

As two men are mentioned this must only refer to homosexuality. One translation says "punish them lightly".

When he tires of one of his wives a Moslem can get rid of her by a mere verbal formula. The SOCIAL LAWS OF THE KORAN says "The ceremony of divorce among Muhammedans is very simple, the husband merely saying 'Thou art divorced' or 'I herewith dismiss thee'." The KORAN does not give a woman the right to a divorce for any reason whatsoever.

Women are also oppressed in other ways, and are regarded as being very much inferior beings. The KORAN says that men are a degree above them and that they should be obedient to their husbands, and that for disloyalty they can be beaten.

THE VEIL

It was Mohammed who imposed the veil on women. Millions of women through large parts of the world in the last 1200 years have never been able to go out without wearing the veil.

I have myself spent 1-1/2 years in Aden, not far south of the area where Mohammed spent his life. I have seen women completely covered with veils that cover their entire faces in humidity so high that as soon as one puts on a shirt it is soaking with sweat. If they had appeard unveiled they would probably have been killed. It is worth noting that the Moslem religion mostly exists in countries that are near the Equator, so this imposition of the veil is not a trivial matter.

CLITORECTOMY

The Islamic law says of circumcision and clitorectomy, "It is an obligation for men and women to do it for themselves and their children, and if they neglect it, the Imam may force them to it for it is right and necessary."

In THE SYDNEY MORNING HERALD of January 16, 1979 there was an article on clitorectomy (female circumcision) in Egypt. Nawal Alsa'adawi, the Egyptian gynaecologist and psychiatrist, was reported to have said: "You can't separate sexual oppression from political and religious oppression."

In an article on the practice it was claimed that nearly all of the young girls in Egyptian villages, where most of the people live, are circumcised. The article went on: "This circumcision is, in effect, castration of women. For the women the pleasure of sex is gone."

Some of the girls bleed to death. Others develop abcesses. The article claimed that the religious establishment found her view too threatening. Nawal defended Islam, and claimed that it was not responsible for these circumcisions, and that Mohammed was progressive in regard to women. I have shown in my section on this that this was not the case. She could hardly do otherwise in a country as religious as Egypt. She has enough of a problem trying to prevent these mutilations from taking place, without challenging the very basis of the religion itself.

WOMEN BEFORE ISLAM

Women had a much higher status in Arabia before Islam. There are accounts of women fighting in battles, riding across the desert, visiting men alone, and taking part in public debates.

Each of these stories ends with the words: "This was before the Apostle received the revelation about veiling." The freedom women enjoyed before Islam is shown by the example of Khadija, Mohammed's first wife. She was an heiress, and business woman, and she proposed to him.

Women took a great part in the opposition to Mohammed. One of his foremost opponents was Hind the wife of Abu Sofian, the leader of the Meccans.

When Mohammed finally marched on Mecca and captured it, Abu Sofian made a speech to the people telling them that it was useless to oppose the Moslems. Hind jumped up beside him and shouted: "Don't take any notice of this fat old fool. A fine protector of his people he is."

A poetess called Asma who lived in Medina wrote some satirical verses, making fun of her fellow citizens' adoption of Mohammed as their religious leader. These were passed from mouth to mouth, holding him up to ridicule. Mohammed arranged for her to be assassinated. She was stabbed in her tent, surrounded by her five children.

INTOLERANCE TOWARDS OTHER RELIGIONS

Islam is the only religion in the world which teaches that converts can be won at the point of a sword. The KORAN says that those who won't accept Islam are to be killed. "When ye encounter the unbelievers, strike off their heads, until ye have made a great slaughter among them."

The KORAN says: "Fight those who believe not in Allah" and that Moslems are to fight against non-believers until "there prevail justice and faith in Allah altogether and every-where." We have already seen what kind of 'justice' exists when Islam is established as the religion of a country.

The KORAN says: "Fighting is prescribed for you, and ye dislike, but it is possible that ye dislike a thing which is good for you." "If anyone desires a religion other than Islam (submission to Allah), never will it be accepted of him." The KORAN continues: "How many populations have we destroyed."

A great deal is made of the tolerance of Islam towards Christianity and Judaism. This is exaggerated. Islam was more tolerant towards these two religions than it was towards paganism, but that is not saying much.

Mohammed regarded the Christian doctrine of the trinity as being the worship of three gods. Also that the central teaching of Christianity--that Jesus is the son of God--is blasphemous. The KORAN says that those who believe these two things will go to hell. The KORAN says: "O ye who believe! Take not the Jews and the Christians for your friends and protectors. They are friends and protectors to each other."

It should be remembered that the Moslems delivered an entirely unprovoked attack on many Christian countries. When they took Christian Constantinople the streets ran with blood. A great part of the Moslem empire consisted of countries that had formerly been Christian.

Just before Mohammed died, he expressed the wish that there "not remain any faith but that of Islam throughout the whole land of Arabia." In accordance with his wishes the Jews and Christians were expelled from that country.

PAGANS ATTACKED

The pagans bore the brunt of Islamic fury. Sir William Muir says of these: ". . .but for the rest the sword is not to be sheathed till they are exterminated, or submit to the faith which has become superior to every other religion."

The KORAN says: ". . .fight and slay the pagans wherever you find them." Another translation says: "Kill those who ascribe partners to God." Again, the KORAN says that pagans are unclean. Other translations use the word 'polytheist' instead of 'pagan' and one translates this verse as 'polytheists are filth'.

This is sometimes considered to be justified as most people are ignorant of the nature of the religion of Arabia before Islam. The image conjured up is of hideous idols, and human sacrifices, and corrupt priesthood. This is not borne out by the facts.

There was no religious prejudice or persecution before Mohammed and charities existed to look after orphans; they also collected money to buy the freedom of slaves.

The Meccans did not turn against him until he attacked their gods, and announced that their ancestors were in hell.

Glubb says that the attitude of the pagans towards their temples and images were similar to that of the British to Westheimer Abbey, and other similar places in England. It is worth noting that there was no priesthood in the paganism of Arabia of the time. Though Islam is not supposed to have priests, the equivalent has developed in most Moslem countries, and a religious establishment has arisen, which in many of them has enormous power. So in this respect Islam was a retrograde step.

Also the god concept of Islam can hardly be an improvement on paganism, as even though Allah is called 'the merciful, the beneficent', this is hardly borne out by his action in torturing all non-believers in hell forever. A description of the Moslem hell will give some idea of the nature of the sort of god they believe in.

THE MOSLEM HELL

In the Moslem hell one's skin is constantly being renewed after being roasted through so the victim can "taste the penalty." They will be wearing a garment of fire. They will eat foul fruits and be made to drink boiling water. Over their heads will be poured boiling water. The water is not just boiling but foetid and "in gulps will he sip it, but never will he be near swallowing down his throat. Death will come to him from every quarter, yet will he not die; and in front of him will be a chastisement unrelenting." It will last forever, and it will not be lightened and he will be in despair. They will beg for death but it will be denied. As if that were not enough--"there will be maces of iron to punish them,"

INDIA

The intolerance of Islam towards polytheism (the worship of more than one god) has drowned the world in blood. This was particularly the case in India. In most parts of the world the pagans found it easier to give in and become Moslems. But the Hindus were prepared to fight.

When the Moslems got to India they attacked the Hindus, killed them, and destroyed their temples and images. In Kanauj alone 10,000 temples were destroyed, and 50,000 Hindus were killed.

The Hindus get on with each other quite well. There has been very little conflict between the various sects of that religion. As far as they are concerned a man can worship anything he wants or nothing at all. Hinduism is very tolerant in the matter of religion.

The religious strife between Moslems and Hindus is still continuing. An eyewitness to the religious fighting during the British Raj states:

"The moment the crowd decided that one of the opposite religion had been killed, then everyone in one form of dress would turn on the others. . . . . .Thousands upon thousands an hour being killed, and of course it was a most terrifying sight. They'd pick up any weapon they could, they shouted, they smashed, they always tried to whittle out the opposition so that they were heavily outnumbered. . .Or you could go across Harrar Bridge, and you could see them being laid on their faces, with their heads poking out over the bridge, and being beheaded into the river, and their bodies being thrown in afterwards. Of course, after the riot the river was practically choked with dead bodies. . ."

In the years since Islam was first established vast numbers of people must have died as a result of its teachings. Glubb estimates that perhaps one or two people might have been killed in a normal Bedoin raid. In the religious wars that took place when Mohammed proclaimed Jihad (holy war) many millions have been killed.

When India was granted independence over 1,000,000 were killed in the strife which broke out between members of the two religions.

Even as I write these words reports are coming in from all over the world--in India, Indonesia, Iran, the Philippines, North Africa--of Moslems fighting each other, and the members of other religions. One does not read of Buddhists, Jains, Parsees fighting members of other religions. It's always the Moslems who are involved--apart from Protestants and Catholics fighting each other in Northern Ireland.

One can only conclude that there is something about this religion that causes this to happen. This is the 'holy' book of Islam, the KORAN, that incites its followers to attack and kill those who belong to other faiths.

THE SUPPRESSION OF KNOWLEDGE

One myth that is widely believed is that Islam promoted knowledge, but this is not the case. In later centuries a high civilisation did develop in Moslem countries, but this was despite Islam, not because of it.

Gibb says: "The struggle to subordinate all intellectual life to the authority of religion went on for many centuries in successive regions of the Muslim world."

In the first and second centuries of Islam "a Moslem's duty was to practice Islam and not medicine." The KORAN and the mosque remained the basis of Arab education until the Abbasids initiated a great age of learning in the 9th century.

Arab civilisation was built on that of Greece, Persia, and Rome. Islam initially set these back. It is said that the Moslems preserved the knowledge of the Greeks, but it was already being kept by the Byzantines, and Moslems merely continued this process. All the evidence indicates that Islam was a danger to Greek thought, and that it was just a lucky accident that it survived at all under this religion.

In 744 the rationalist Caliph Yazid III decreed that the doctrine of predestination should give way to that of free will. Then in 762 the capital of Islam was moved to Baghdad, in Persia, and civilisation began again to flourish in the middle east. This owed more to the ancient civilisation of Persia, which had already been 1,000 years old when Mohammad was born, than it did to Islam.

"......Persian songs, as well as Persian ideas and thoughts, won the day...and paved the way for a new era distinguished by the cultivation of science and scholarly pursuits."

The Islamic world has sunk back into ignorance again, and even in such great universities as Al-Azhar at Cairo--the largest Moslem university in the world--the KORAN is the basis of education. In many schools the children learn nothing else. The KORAN remains the basis of the law, and the foundation of the Moslem legal, judicial, and political system, and the guide to every aspect of life.

ISLAM UNDEMOCRATIC

Another myth about Islam is that it promoted equality. In reality Islam permitted the ultimate inequality--slavery.

As Muir says of Mohammed: "He rivetted the fetter." "There is no obligation whatever on a Moslem to release his slaves." Mohammed himself had slaves--17 men and 11 women.

One of the early Caliphs, Omar "insisted on a medieval Apartheid with the Arabs as master race."

In subsequent years the Arabs had one of the worst records as slavers, and this has continued right up till the later years of the 20th century and may still be going on. Some of the worst feudal regimes in history were based on Islam as is the present regime in Saudi Arabia.

Mohammed himself set a procedure for this by ruling Arabia as absolute dictator. Nutting says: "Mohammed concentrated all power, temporal and spiritual in his own hands, and had combined in himself the offices of lawgiver, chief judge, and commander, head of state and head of church."

He never bothered (or Allah never revealed to him) to convey the method by which he was to be succeeded. After his death this led to the bloody wars between the Shi'ite and Sunni Moslems.

DON'T PRAY FOR RELATIVES

On returning from a raid against a tribe called the Banu Lahyan, Mohammed stopped at the grave of his mother. The following 'revelation' prevented him from praying for her soul: "It is not fitting for the Prohet and those who believe, that they should pray for forgiveness for pagans, even though they be next of kin. . . . ."

CRUELTY TO ANIMALS

According to Moslem halal rites, when any animal is slaughtered, the man who kills it must face towards Mecca, and say a prayer when he cuts its throat. It is essential for the animal to bleed to death, and it must be fully conscious, and cannot be tranquilized, or stunned.

ISLAM GROVELLING

The very essence of Islam is a supine acceptance of a grovelling acceptance of one's lot. The word 'Islam' itself means submission. That is the will of Allah. They believe that nothing happens without His permission, so there is no point in trying to do anything about improving this life.

The doctrine of predestination is taught in the KORAN, 9.51 and in other passages.

ISLAM AND ART

Islam had a bad effect on art, as Mohammed disliked painting, music and poetry. Luckily, the liking of the Arabs for the last two of these was too great for his influence to have much effect. It was on painting and sculpture that Islam had the worst influence, as all representations of either human or animal forms were forbidden, so their art was restricted to mindless patterns.

Mohammed said that those who decorate their tombs and churches with paintings "were the worst part of all creation."

MOHAMMED

The example of the life of Mohammed is taken, with the KORAN, as a guide to how life should be lived. It is therefore very important to consider his character, and acts. When I began writing this pamphlet, I did not think that I would like Mohammed. But the more I read about him the less attractive did I find him.

He was guilty of the worst crimes any man can commit-- murder. On one occasion he had the entire male population of a Jewish tribe, the Bani Quraizah, massacred and then had the women and children sold into slavery. Every book on Mohammed mentions this incident, and the KORAN, 33.26 refers to it.

Mohammed had people killed for the most trivial reasons. A man called Kinana ibn Ali al Huquiq, who was the leader of a Jewish tribe whose fort was captured by the Moslems, tried to conceal the fact that he had gold. When an informer told Mohammed of this he had Kinana tortured by having hot coals put on his chest till he was nearly dead, and then he was killed.

A man called Al Nadhr, who was a teller of tales, used to say of Mohammed to his audiences: "Are not my stories as good as his?" For this Mohammed orderd that his head be struck off. After the battle of Badr a man called Uqba was taken prisoner. When he was being taken away to be executed, he said to Mohammed: "What will become of my little children." Mohammed replied: Hellfire."

It might be thought that I am quoting from books which are hostile to Mohammed. This is not so. Only Muir's book is slightly hostile to him. All the others go out of their way to portray him in a favourable light. We have enough evidence in the KORAN of Mohammed's cruel nature, in the punishments he ordered, his descriptions of hell, and his incitements to his followers to kill people.

Though he ordered the horrible mutilation of the cutting off of hands for theft, he was himself one of the biggest thieves in history. A 'revelation' from Allah permitted Mohammed to keep one-fifth of the spoils captured from the towns his followers invaded, and the caravans they raided.

He was incredibly prudish. At Medina it was the practice to fertilise the female date palm tree by hand. Mohammed was so disgusted by this that he forbade his followers to practice it. The result was that hardly any of the trees bore fruit, so he had to rescind his order.

At the same time he was extremely lecherous, as can be seen by the large number of wives he had. Karl Brookelmann, in his book, HISTORY OF THE ISLAMIC PEOPLES, says that Mohammed's death was brought on by "an excess of pleasure-taking in the harem."

The only thing that can be said in his favour was that he did on occasion refrain from killing people. I can't myself see that to be a particularly great virtue.

It might be wondered how a man with this sort of character could become so admired, and could attain the position he did. What is not realised is that many people of the time detested him.

After ten years of preaching in Mecca he only had acquired 70 followers. When he secured a base at Medina, he used the same methods as Hitler or the American gangster Al Capone to establish his religion. All the accounts that tell us of him are biased in his favour, as death or exile awaited anyone who criticised Mohammed or the KORAN when Islam became the state religion of Arabia.

It might be said that Mohammed was a man of his time. but we must judge him according to the standards of today, not those of 1200 years ago. We should try to improve on the ethics of the past. Moslems claim that Islam is a religion for our time, and it is by the ideals of this century that we should measure it, not by those of the 7th century.

According to these standards Mohammed was a cruel barbarian, merciless and fanatical. He introduced religious hatred into large parts of the world that before were tolerant on such matters. He curtailed the freedom of women. He endorsed slavery. He broke up families. He ordered cruel punishments. The world would have been a better place if he had never been born.

From publication of the Rationalist Association of N.S.W.
58 Regent Street, Chippendale, N.S.W. 2008, Australia.

(By H. L. Oberoi and P. N. Oak)

A GLIMPSE OF PRE-ISLAMIC ARABIA

Arabia is an abbreviation. The original word even today is Arbasthan. It originates in Arvasthan. As observed earlier Sanskrit "V" changes into "B". Arva in Sanskrit means a horse. Arvasthan signifies a land of horses, and as we all know Arabia is famous for its horses.

In the 6th and 7th centuries A.D. a wave of effecting a complete break with the past spread over West Asia. All links with the past were broken, images smashed, scriptures destroyed, education discontinued and the entire West Asian region took a plunge in abyssmal ignorance which lasted for centuries thereafter and perhaps persists to a certain extent even today because if in the whole world modern scientific and educational developments find stubborn and entrenched resistance anywhere it is in the West Asian countries. It is said that the late Saudi Arabia ruler could not permit a radio broadcasting station opened in his own capital because of oposition from his Maulavis. He then resorted to a strategem. Once while he had his council of Maulavis in attendance he had a radio set switched on to a program of Koranic recitation broadcast from a small transmitting station set up earlier without much ado. The Maulavis were delighted, so goes the report, to hear the word of Allah coming to them as if from nowhere. The king told them that what objections could they have to a mechanism which broadcast the word of Allah. The Maulavis agreed and the small radio broadcasting project was at last ratified.

According to Encyclopaedia Britannica and Encyclopaedia Islamia the Arabs are ignorant of their own history of the pre-Muslim era. By a strange euphemism they call it a period of ignorance and darkness. Probably no other country in the world has deliberately written off a 2,500 year period of their own history by systematically stamping out and snapping all links with the past. They have wiped the memories of pre-Muslim era off their minds. So while they chose to remain ignorant of their past ironically enough it is they who dub the pre-Muslim era as a period of ignorance.

Fortunately we can still trace the history of that pre-Islamic Arabia. It is a well known adage that there is no such thing as foolproof destruction of all evidence. The pre-Islamic history of Arabia is the story of Indian Kshatriyas over that land, with the people following the Vedic way of life.

In our attempt to reconstruct the story of pre-Islamic Arabia we begin with the name of the country itself. As explained earlier the name is fully Sanskrit. Its central pilgrim centre, Mecca is also a Sanskrit name. Makha in Sanskrit signifies a sacrificial fire. Since Vedic fire worship was prevalent all over West Asia in pre-Islamic days Makha signifies the place which had an important shrine of fire worship.

Coinciding with the annual pilgrimage of huge bazaar used to spring up in Makha i.e. Mecca since times immemorial. The annual pilgrimage of Muslims to Mecca is not at all an innovation but a continuation of the ancient pilgrimage. This fact is mentioned in encyclopaedias.

VIKRAMADITYA

Evidence is now available that the whole of Arabia was part of the great Indian King Vikramaditya's vast empire. The extent of Vikramaditya's empire is one of the main reasons for his world wide fame. Incidentally this also explains many intriguing features about Arabia. It could be that Vikramaditya himself had this peninsula named Arvasthan if he was the first Indian monarch to capture it and bring it under his sway.

The second intriguing aspect is the existence of a Shivalinga or the Mahadeva emblem in the Kaaba shrine in Mecca. Before going into further details about the ancient Vedic rituals and names still clinging to Muslim worship at Mecca we shall see what evidence we have about Arabia having formed part of Vikramaditya's dominions.

ANTHOLOGY OF ANCIENT ARABIC POETRY: SAYAR-UL-OKUL

In Istanbul in Turkey, there is a famous library called Makteb-e-Sultania which is reputed to have the largest collection of ancient West Asian literature. In the Arabic Section of that library is an anthology of ancient Arabic poetry. That anthology was compiled from an earlier work in A.D. 1742 under the orders of the Turkish ruler Sultan Salim.

The 'pages' of that volume are made of HAREER - a kind of silk used for writing on. Each page has a decorative gilded border. It may be recalled that gilding pages of sacred books is an ancient custom associated with old Sanskrit scriptures found in Java and other places. The anthology itself is known as SAYAR-UL-OKUL. It is divided into three parts, the first part contains biographic details and the poetic compositions of pre-Islamic Arabian poets. The second part embodies accounts and verses of poets of the period beginning just after Prophet Mohammad up to the end of Banee - Ummayya dynasty. The third part deals with later poets up to the end of Khalifa Harun-al-Rashid's times. Incidentally "Banee" means "Vanee" and Ummayya as in Krishnayya are Sanskrit names.

Abu Amir Abdul Asamai, a distinguished Arabian bard who was the Poet Laureate of Harun-al--Rashid's court has compiled and edited the anthology.

The first modern edition of Sayar-ul-Okul anthology was printed and published in Berlin in A.D. 1864. A subsequent edition was published in Beirut in A.D. 1932. This work is regarded as the most important and authoritative anthology of ancient Arabic poetry. It throws considerable light on the social life, customs, manners and entertainment forms in ancient Arabia. The book also contains an elaborate description of the ancient Mecca shrine, the town and the annual fair known as OKAJ which used to be held there every year. This should convince readers that the annual Haj of the Muslims to the Kaaba is only a continuation of the old fair and not a new practice.

But the OKAJ fair was far from a carnival. It provided a forum for the elite and learned to discuss the social, religious, political, literary and other aspects of the Vedic culture then pervading Arabia. Sayar-ul-Okul asserts that the conclusions reached at those discussions were widely respected througout Arabia. Mecca, therefore, followed the Varanasi tradition of providing a seat for important discussions among the learned while the masses congregated there for spiritual bliss. The principal shrines at both Varanasi in India and at Mecca in Arvasthan were Shiva temples. Even to this day the central object of veneration at both Mecca and Varanasi continues to be the ancient Mahadeva emblems. It is the Shankara stone which Muslim pilgrims reverently touch and kiss in the Kaaba.

ENTRY OF NON-MUSLIMS FORBIDDEN

A few miles away from Mecca is a big signboard which forbids entry to any non-Muslim in the area.   This is a reminder of the days when the Shrine was stormed and captured solely for the newly established faith of Islam. The object obviously was to prevent its recaptue.

As the pilgrim proceeds towards Mecca he is asked to shave his head and beard and to don a special sacred attire. This consists of two seamless sheets of white cloth. One is to be worn round the waist and the other over the shoulders. Both these rites are remnants of the old Vedic practice of entering Hindu shrines, clean shaven and with holy seamless spotless white sheets.

The main shrine in Mecca which houses the Shiva emblem is known as the Kaaba. It is clothed in a black shroud. This custom could also originate from the days when it was thought necessary to discourage its recapture. According to encyclopaedias Britannica and Islamia the Kaaba had 360 images. Traditional accounts mention that one of the deities among the 360 destroyed, when the shrine was stormed, was that of Saturn, another was of the moon and yet another was one called Allah. In India the practice of Navagraha puja that is worship of the nine planets is still in vogue. Two of these nine are the Saturn and the moon. Besides, the moon is always associated with Lord Shankara. A Crescent is always painted across the forehead of the Shiva emblem. Since the presiding deity at the Kaaba shrine was Lord Shiva i.e. Shankara, the crescent was also painted on it. It is that crescent which is now adopted as a religious symbol of Islam. Another Hindu tradition is that wherever there is a Shiva shrine the sacred stream of Ganga that is the Ganges must also co-exist. True to that tradition a sacred fount exists near the Kaaba. Its water is held sacred because it was regarded as but another Ganga since pre-Islamic times. Muslim pilgrims visiting the Kaaba shrine go around it seven times. In no other mosque does this perambulation prevail. Hindus invariably perambulate around their shrines. This is yet another proof that the Kaaba shrine is a pre-Islamic Shiva temple where the Hindu practice of perambulation is still meticulously observed.

Allah is a Sanskrit word. In Sanskrit Allah, Akka and Amba are synonyms. They signify a goddess or mother. The term Allah appears in Sanskrit chants while invoking goddess Durga i.e. Bhavani. The Islamic word Allah for God is therefore not an innovation but the ancient Sanskrit appellation retained and continued to be used by Islam.

The seven perambulations too are significant. At Hindu wedding ceremonies the bride and bridegroom go round the sacred fire seven times. the practice of seven perambultions around the Kaaba shrine in Mecca is, therefore, a Hindu Vedic custom. It is also a proof that Mecca was Makha or the shrine of the sacred fire around which worshippers made seven perambulations.

SAYAR-UL-OKUL tells us that a pan-Arabic poetic symposium used to be held in Mecca at the annual Okaj fair in pre-Islamic times. All leading poets used to participate in it. Poems considered best were awarded prizes. The best poems engraved on gold plate were hung inside the temple. Others etched on camel or goat skin were hung outside. Thus for thousands of years the Kaaba was the treasure house of the best Arabian poetic thought. This tradition was of immemorial antiquity. But most of the poems got lost and destroyed during the storming of the Kaaba by prophet Mohammed's forces.

SAYAR-UL-OKUL is a poem by UMAR-BINE-HASSNAM (Poetic Title: ABBUL-HIQAM meaning Father of Knowledge). He was an uncle of prophet Mohammed. He refused to get converted to Islam. He died a martyr at the hands of Muslim fanatics who wanted to wipe out non-Muslims. This poem was adjudged as the best in the annual fair at Kaaba.

QAFA VINAK ZIQRA MIN ULUMIN TAV
ASERU KALUBAN AYATTUL HAWA VA TAZAKKARU

A man who has spent all his life in sin and immorality and has wasted away his life in passion and fury,

VA TAZAKEROHA AUDAN ELALVADAE LILVARA
VALUK YANE ZATULLA HE YOM TAB ASERU

If he repents in the end and wants to return to morality, is there a way for his redemption?

VA AHLOLAHA AZAHU ARMIMAN MAHADEV O
MANAZEL ILAMUDDINE MINJUM VA SAYATTARU

Even if only once he sincerely worships Mahadeva, he can attain the highest position in the path of righteousness.

VA SAHABI KEYAM FEEM QAMIL HINDE YOMAN
VA YAQULOON LATAHAZAN FAINNAK TAVAJJARU

Oh Lord! Take away all my life and in return pray grant me even a single day's stay in Hind (India) as a man becomes spiritually free on reaching that holy land.

MAYASSAYARE AKHALAQAN HASNAN KULLAHUM
NAJUMUN AZAAT SUMM GABUL HINDU

By dint of a pilgrimage of Hind a man attains the merit of noble deeds and gets the privilege of pious touch with ideal Hindu teachers.

Footnote

1.   Shankara: another name of Hindu god Shiva.

Bibliography

GOEL, Sita Ram: Hindu Society Under Siege/Islamic Imperialism In India/Defense Of Hindu Society/Genesis And History Of The Politics Of Conversion (all published by the Voice of India, New Delhi)

SWARUP, Ram: Understanding Islam through Hadis (published by Exposition Press, New York)

OAK, P. N.: The Taj Mahal is Tejo Mahalaya - A Shiva Temple (published by the Author, New Delhi)

SARKAR, Sir Jadu Nath: History of Aurangzib (Volumes I-V)/Fall of the Mughal Empire (Volumes I-IV)/Mughal Administration/Shivaji and his Times (published by Orient Longman, New Delhi)

SRIVASTAVA, A. L.: The Sultanate of Delhi/The Mughal Empire (published by Shiva Lal Agarwala & Co, Agra)

MUTHANNA, I. M.: Tipu Sultan X'Rayed (published by the Author)

PATAI, Raphael: The Arab Mind (published by Charles Schribner's Sons, New York)

GARDNER, Brian: The East India Company (published by the McCall Publishing Company, New York)

SWAMI, Vivekananda: The Complete Works (published by Advaita Ashrama, Calcutta)

MASTERS, R. E. L./LEA, Eduard: Sex Crimes in History (published by Matrix House, New York)

GROUSSET, René: The Epic of the Crusades (published by Orion Press, New York)

168

McDONALD, John: Flight from Dhahran (Published by Prentice-Hall, Inc. Englewood Cliffs, N.J.)

AL GHAZZALI: Nasihat Al-Muluk

OLSEN, Viggo: DAKTAR - Diplomat in Bangladesh (published by Moody Press, Chicago)

SMITH, Vincent A.: Akbar the Great Mogul (published by S. Chand & Co, New Delhi)

PENZER, N. M.: The Harem (published by Spring Books, London)

GHOSH, Shailendra Kumar: Gaud Kahini (in Bengali) (published by D. M. Library, Calcutta)

AL-SIDDIQUI, Maulvi K.: Bahr-ul-Ulum (in Bengali) (published by Gausia Library, Calcutta)

LACEY, Robert: The Kingdom (published by Harcourt Brace Jovanovich, New York)

LAHIRY, Ashutosh: Gandhi in Indian Politics (published by Firma KLM Pvt Ltd, Calcutta)

KHOMEINI, Imam: Islam and Revolution (Translated and Annotated by Hamid Algar) (published by Mizan Press, Berkeley, California)

SWAMI, Satyanada Saraswati: Anandamather Siddhasadhak /Shaktivad (in Bengali) (published by Shaktivad Math, Garia, West Bengal)

DAWOOD, N. J.: The Koran (published by Penguin Books)

PICKTHALL, Mohammed M.: The Meaning of the Glorious Koran (published by World Islamic Publications, Delhi)

ALI, A. Yusuf: The Holy Quran (published by American Trust Publications, USA)

OBEROI, H. L., OAK, P. N.: A Glimpse of Pre-Islamic Arabia

OAK, P. N.: Christian and Islamic Doomsdays (published by Masurashram Patrika, Goregaon, Bombay)

MAINE, Colin: The Dead Hand of Islam (published by the Rationalist Association of N.S.W., Australia)

SHARIF, Mohammad: Crimes and Punishment in Islam (published by Institute of Islamic Culture, Lahore)

NIAZI, Kausar: Role of the Mosque (published by Sh. Muhammad Ashraf, Lahore)

IDRIS, Gaafar Sheikh: The Process of Islamization (published by the Muslim Students' Association of the U.S.)

A'LA MAUDUDI, S. Abul: Jihad in Islam (published by Islamic Publications Ltd, Lahore)

DASGUPTA, Sukharanjan: Midnight Massacre in Dacca (published by Vikas Publishing House Pvt Ltd, New Delhi)

ASHOK, Parivrajak: Manush, Mushalman o Marxvadi (in Bengali) (Hindusabhyata Prachar o Punarvasan Mahasangha)

ROY, Shivprasad: Divyagnan Noy Kandajnan Chai (In Bengali) (published by Prerana Prakashani, Calcutta)

The picture of the Taj Mahal or Tejo Mahalaya - a Shiva Temple has been taken from the July page of 1983 calendar issued by the hermitage of Swami Amarjyoti, Gold Hill, Salina Star Route, Boulder, Colorado 80302.

SHESHADRI, H. V.: The Tragic Story of Partition (published by Jagarana Prakashan, Bangalore)

News Items from the Illustrated Weekly of India, February 27, 1983.

WALLACE, Irving et al: The Intimate Sex Lives of Famous People (published by Dell Publishing Co., Inc. N.Y.)